BUZZ BUZZ!

Playwrights, Actors and Directors at the National Theatre

JONATHAN CROALL comes from a theatre background: his father, John Stuart, was an actor, and his mother, Barbara Francis, a voice coach. Before becoming a full-time writer he worked as an editor in book publishing and newspapers. He is the author of *Gielgud: A Theatrical Life*; *The Coming of Godot: A Short History of a Masterpiece* (nominated for the 2006 Theatre Book Prize); and three books in the series 'The National Theatre at Work': *Hamlet Observed*, *Peter Hall's 'Bacchai'* and *Inside the Molly House*. His other books include the oral history *Don't You Know There's a War On? Voices from the Home Front*, the biography *Neill of Summerhill: The Permanent Rebel* and a children's novel, *Sent Away*. He currently edits the programmes at the Old Vic and was editor of the National Theatre's *StageWrite* magazine from 1992 to 2007. His authorised biography *Sybil Thorndike: A Star of Life* was published in autumn 2008.

D0784452

POLONIUS The actors are come hither, my lord.

HAMLET   Buzz Buzz!

BUZZ BUZZ!

Playwrights, Actors and Directors at the National Theatre

Interviewed by Jonathan Croall

Methuen Drama

Published by Methuen Drama

10 9 8 7 6 5 4 3 2 1

First published 2008

Methuen Drama
A & C Black Publishers Limited
38 Soho Square
London W1D 3HB
www.acblack.com

Copyright © Jonathan Croall 2008

Jonathan Croall has asserted his rights under the Copyright, Designs and
Patents Act, 1988, to be identified as the author of this work

A CIP catalogue record for this book is available from the British Library

ISBN 978 1 408 10520 7

Typeset in Plantin by SX Composing DTP, Rayleigh, Essex

Printed and bound in Great Britain by Caligraving Ltd, Thetford,
Norfolk

This book is produced using paper that is made from wood grown in
managed, sustainable forests. It is natural, renewable and recyclable. The
logging and manufacturing processes conform to the environmental
regulations of the country of origin.

Contents

Introduction   1

Part One **Playwrights on Their Plays**

Alan Bennett, *The History Boys*   7
Tom Stoppard, *The Coast of Utopia*   9
Tony Kushner, *Angels in America*   13
Pam Gems, *Stanley*   15
Michael Frayn, *Democracy*   16
Joe Penhall, *Landscape with Weapon*   18
Bryony Lavery, *Frozen*   20
Christopher Hampton, *The Talking Cure*   22
Martin McDonagh, *The Cripple of Inishmaan*   25
Rebecca Lenkiewicz, *The Night Season*   26
David Hare, *The Permanent Way*   30
April De Angelis, *A Laughing Matter*   32
Kwame Kwei-Armah, *Fix Up*   34
Michael Frayn, *Copenhagen*   37
Nick Darke, *The Riot*   39
Charlotte Jones, *Humble Boy*   41
Martin Crimp, *Attempts on her Life*   42
Alan Ayckbourn, *Mr A's Amazing Maze Plays*   44
David Hare, *Racing Demon, Murmuring Judges,*
    The Absence of War   47
Hanif Kureishi, *Sleep With Me*   49
Matthew Bourne, *Play Without Words*   51
Jim Cartwright, *The Rise and Fall of Little Voice*   52
Winsome Pinnock, *Leave Taking*   54
Sebastian Barry, *Our Lady of Sligo*   56
David Eldridge, *Market Boy*   57
Nick Stafford, *Battle Royal*   60
Patrick Marber, *Dealer's Choice* and Paul Godfrey,
    The Blue Ball   62

Part Two **Adaptations and Musicals**

Remembrance of Things Past Harold Pinter		67
Coram Boy Helen Edmundson, Melly Still		70
The Canterbury Tales Prunella Scales		73
My Fair Lady Jonathan Pryce		75
War Horse Michael Morpurgo		78
Waves Katie Mitchell		80
The Prime of Miss Jean Brodie Phyllida Lloyd,		
Fiona Shaw		83
Out of a House Walked a Man Simon McBurney		85
Rafta, Rafta . . . Ayub Khan-Din		87
The UN Inspector David Farr		89
A Funny Thing Happened on the Way to the		
Forum Desmond Barrit		91
Tristan & Yseult Emma Rice		93
Theatre of Blood Phelim McDermott		95
War and Peace Helen Edmundson		97
Jerry Springer – The Opera Richard Thomas,		
Stewart Lee		99
Billy Liar Willis Hall, Keith Waterhouse, Tim Supple		100
Dragon Ultz		102

Part Three **Actors and Directors at Work**

THE GREEKS AND SHAKESPEARE

Euripides, *Bacchai* Peter Hall	107
Aristophanes, *Frogs* Fiona Laird	109
Aeschylus, *The Oresteia* Katie Mitchell	111
Hamlet Simon Russell Beale	114
Othello David Harewood	116
Antony and Cleopatra Sean Mathias, Helen Mirren	118
The Winter's Tale Nicholas Hytner	122
Henry IV Matthew Macfadyen	124
Henry V Adrian Lester	126
Measure for Measure Simon McBurney,	
Paul Rhys, Naomi Frederick	128

ENGLISH AND IRISH CLASSICS

Ben Jonson, *Volpone*   Matthew Warchus   133
George Etherege, *The Man of Mode*   Nicholas Hytner   135
William Congreve, *The Way of the World*   Phyllida
    Lloyd   136
Oliver Goldsmith, *She Stoops to Conquer*   Max
    Stafford-Clark   138
Edward Bulwer-Lytton, *Money*   John Caird   139
Bernard Shaw, *Widowers' Houses*   Fiona Shaw   141
Harley Granville Barker, *The Voysey Inheritance*
    Peter Gill, Dominic West, Nancy Carroll   143
J. M. Barrie, *Peter Pan*   Ian McKellen   148
Bernard Shaw, *Saint Joan*   Marianne Elliott,
    Anne-Marie Duff   150

EUROPEAN DRAMA

Pierre Marivaux, *The False Servant*   Charlotte
    Rampling   153
Emile Zola, *Thérèse Raquin*   Marianne Elliott   154
Henrik Ibsen, *An Enemy of the People*   Ian McKellen   155
Henrik Ibsen, *Pillars of the Community*
    Marianne Elliott, Lesley Manville   158
Anton Chekhov, *The Seagull*   Ben Whishaw   162
Edmond Rostand, *Cyrano de Bergerac*   Stephen Rea   163
Anton Chekhov, *Three Sisters*   Eve Best   164
August Strindberg, *A Dream Play*   Katie Mitchell,
    Angus Wright   166
Bertolt Brecht, *Mother Courage and Her Children*
    Anthony Clark   176
Bertolt Brecht, *Mother Courage and Her Children*
    Diana Rigg   177
Bertolt Brecht, *The Life of Galileo*   Howard Davies
    The Caucasian Chalk Circle, Sean Holmes   179

MODERN AMERICAN DRAMA

Sophie Treadwell, *Machinal*   Stephen Daldry,
    Fiona Shaw   182

Contents

Eugene O'Neill, *Mourning Becomes Electra*
Howard Davies, Tim Pigott-Smith 184
Arthur Miller, *All My Sons* Julie Walters 192
Arthur Miller, *Death of a Salesman* David Thacker 195
Sam Shepard, *Buried Child* Matthew Warchus,
Lauren Ambrose 196
David Mamet, *Edmond* Edward Hall,
Kenneth Branagh 198

MODERN ENGLISH AND IRISH DRAMA
Samuel Beckett, *Happy Days* Fiona Shaw 202
Brian Friel, *Aristocrats* Tom Cairns, Peter McDonald,
Dervla Kirwan, Andrew Scott, Gina McKee 204
Christopher Hampton, *Alice's Adventures Under
Ground* Martha Clarke 206
Tom Stoppard, *Rosencrantz and Guildenstern Are Dead*
Simon Russell Beale 208
David Hare, *Skylight* Stella Gonet 209
Nicholas Wright, *Vincent in Brixton* Jochum Ten
Haaf 210
Moira Buffini, *Dinner* Harriet Walter 212
Owen McCafferty, *Scenes from the Big Picture*
Peter Gill 213
Nick Dear, *Power* Robert Lindsay 215
Martin McDonagh, *The Pillowman* David Tennant 217
David Hare, *Stuff Happens* Nicholas Farrell,
Alex Jennings 218
Philip Pullman, *His Dark Materials* David Harewood 220
Harold Pinter, *The Hothouse* Ian Rickson 222

Introduction

Between 1992 and 2007, under the successive directorships of Richard Eyre, Trevor Nunn and Nicholas Hytner, the National Theatre drew to London's South Bank the cream of the country's theatrical talent. During those years, as editor at various times of three of the National's magazines, I was able to interview a good many of the leading playwrights, actors and directors as they went about their work.

Some I talked to before rehearsals began; others offered their impressions and opinions hot from the rehearsal room; a few were able to discuss their work after the play's opening night. We met in dressing rooms, in rehearsal rooms, in a tiny room in the National's press department or, just occasionally, in their own homes. In these relaxed settings they talked freely about the pleasures and problems of working in the theatre, and specifically about their involvement in shows at the National.

With the playwrights I interviewed the focus was on the process of writing, their methods of research, their role in rehearsals, and their ways of collaborating with their directors. Why did Tom Stoppard end up writing three plays for *The Coast of Utopia*? What inspired Kwame Kwei-Armah to write about the Black British experience? Why did Pam Gems choose a painter she both loved and hated in creating *Stanley*? Why is Michael Blakemore so valuable as a director to Michael Frayn? The answers to these and scores of other questions provided an absorbing glimpse into the creative life of these twenty-six very different playwrights.

Adapting existing material for the stage is another kind of exercise from original creation. So it was fascinating to discover how Harold Pinter distilled the essence of Proust's epic novel for *Remembrance of Things Past*; how Emma Rice and Kneehigh Theatre transformed a famous Cornish love story into their innovative *Tristan & Yseult*; why Ayub

1

Khan-Din chose to set a Bill Naughton story in a different culture for his *Rafta, Rafta . . .* It was equally instructive to hear how Helen Edmundson took apart and put together again works as diverse as *War and Peace* and *Coram Boy.*

More than half of the book is devoted to interviews with leading actors and directors. With the actors I was intrigued to discover how Simon Russell Beale prepared to get inside Hamlet's mind; why Helen Mirren was tackling Cleopatra for the third time; what Anne-Marie Duff felt about taking on Shaw's feisty Saint Joan; why playing Captain Hook in *Peter Pan* was a mixed blessing for Ian McKellen; how Diana Rigg was determined to have fun with Mother Courage. These and the many other actors I talked to were pleasingly willing to share their ideas, about their character, the art and craft of acting, and their style of collaboration with their director.

The directors themselves offered valuable insights into the plays, as well as snapshots of their work in the rehearsal room, their reasons for casting the leading parts, and much else. I heard from Nicholas Hytner about his fresh and illuminating approach to *The Winter's Tale* and Shakespeare generally; listened to Peter Hall outline his passionate belief in the use of masks for *Bacchai*; discovered why Marianne Elliott gave Ibsen a makeover in *Pillars of the Community*; and learnt about the great pioneer Granville Barker and the virtues of *The Voysey Inheritance* from Peter Gill. It was rewarding also to be able to talk in greater detail to Katie Mitchell about her radical approach to Strindberg's *A Dream Play*, and to Howard Davies about the huge challenge he faced in directing Eugene O'Neill's epic *Mourning Becomes Electra.*

Some of the pieces I wrote as conventional features, filling in background and context. In others I simply allowed the persons concerned to speak for themselves. Just occasionally, with the longer interviews, I used our conversation verbatim. I hope together they will provide a valuable record of the dazzling variety of work staged at the National during these years by many of the theatre's most creative artists.

While most of the pieces were published in *StageWrite*, the magazine of the National's education department, a few appeared in publications from other departments. I am indebted for their help to several people at the National: to Jenny Harris, Breda Daly, Clare O'Brien and Vivien Wallace for commissioning the pieces, to Lucinda Morrison and Mary Parker for setting up many of the interviews, to Lyn Haill for helping me to get the book published, and to Emma Gosden, Sarah Clarke, Christopher Walters and Charlotte Wilkinson for help in accessing the material. Finally, I'd like to thank Mark Dudgeon at Methuen Drama for agreeing to publish the book, and Ilsa Yardley for editing the text.

Part One

Playwrights on Their Plays

Playing the knowledge game

Alan Bennett discusses the ideas behind
The History Boys

The play is set in a school in the North. One of the characters is Scripps, a devout sixth-former who aspires to be a writer. Reading the play for the first time, its director Nicholas Hytner took this to be a self-portrait. Its author wishes it were: 'I was a religious boy, it's true, but I was also conservative and censorious, and nowhere near as sceptical, open-minded and generally sensible as Scripps.'

In the warm, cluttered study of his north London house – where there's now a car in the drive instead of a lady in a van – Alan Bennett talks eloquently about his time at Leeds Modern Boys' School, his feelings about examinations, his opinions on history teaching, and the origins of his new play at the National.

The History Boys revolves around a bunch of sixth-formers trying for Oxbridge. Some fifty years ago Bennett went through the same experience. Today he still remembers the culture shock of arriving in Cambridge for three days of exams and interviews. 'To somebody coming from a dark industrial northern town, the place itself was magical. But when you saw the assurance of the public-school candidates, you felt you were an interloper. I'd never been exposed to them before, and I was startled at how oafish and self-confident they were. That was quite daunting.'

He ended up at Oxford, as an undergraduate at Exeter College, then a junior history don at Magdalen. But the injustice of a divided educational system that favoured the well-off still rankles. 'People very seldom got into Oxford from my school. It just wasn't geared to it: none of the masters knew what papers you took, or the kind of questions you might be asked; you just had to work it out for yourself. I remember thinking, perhaps for the first time, that this was unfair. Still, at that time more and more state schools were sending their pupils to the older universities, so the imbalance looked like

7

being redressed. Not any more, I'm afraid, and top-up fees won't help.'

While his 1968 play *Forty Years On* was a very literary work ('It came out of my reading rather than my experience'), *The History Boys* is more personal and more serious, raising questions about the conflict between culture, education and schooling, how history (including the Holocaust) should be taught, and the humanising effect of poetry. It centres on the clash between the bow-tied, anti-exam, maverick English teacher Hector ('Set Aside, that's what my lessons are') and the young, more worldly supply teacher Irwin, with Mrs Lintott, a conventional but reliable history teacher, caught in between. Pressurising them all to deliver results is the anxious Headmaster ('I am thinking league tables, targets, customer base, classroom control').

Bennett is reluctant to define the essence of the play. 'It's hard to say what it's about until the actors rehearse it, and then you find out. But it certainly wasn't my views about education that made me write it. I suppose it's more to do with attitudes to knowledge, although that perhaps makes it sound too theoretical: the characters are what it's about; plays always start from the characters.'

Theoretical his play isn't: while it brims with ideas and intellectual arguments, it's also full of good jokes, witty exchanges and idiosyncratic characters of all ages. Bennett says that none of the teachers is based on any that he knew personally, but that Hector was partly inspired by charismatic ones he has read about. Irwin's attitude to exams, on the other hand, 'is to do with my own self-developed technique for passing them, both when I was applying for university and when I took my degree'.

He confesses to anxiety about writing the teenage characters. 'I don't really know what boys of seventeen are like, so I think it would be very short-sighted to plunder their language or their attitudes, to kit them out with all the contemporary speech clichés. But somehow you've to make it appropriate – which is another reason why you wait for rehearsals, when you can find out what they're like, and see what their attitudes are.'

He happily acknowledges the help he's had from Nicholas Hytner, who also directed *The Lady in the Van*, *The Madness of George III* and his adaptation of *The Wind in the Willows*. 'Nick is very articulate about what's wrong with a play. Directing can be a lazy profession, but he never stops working on the text. He's also as concerned about an actor on the edge of a scene as one in the centre, and that's very rare. And – this might seem a criticism, but it's the reverse – he has a streak of showbiz vulgarity, which I don't have and which I think is priceless. He's capable of the broad strokes.'

Like most playwrights, Bennett enjoys rehearsals – 'It's about the only time I get out of the house really.' But he doesn't go as often as he used to do. 'If very precise northern speech is called for I'd go every day, simply to keep an eye on it. But that's not the case here. Anyway, I'm hardly an intimidating presence. At the rehearsals for *The Madness of George III* one actor, Anthony Calf, would greet my arrival with, "Here comes the geography master again!"'

The History Boys opened in the Lyttelton in May 2004.

The Russians are coming

Tom Stoppard talks for the first time about his epic trilogy *The Coast of Utopia*

To write one play for the National may be regarded as good fortune; to write three looks like recklessness. Tom Stoppard half agrees. 'I'm not sure if I would have got into this if I'd realised it would turn into a trilogy,' he says, only half jokingly, as we talk on the eve of rehearsals.

He had the idea of writing a play about nineteenth-century Russian revolutionary figures nearly five years ago, soon after *The Invention of Love*, his last play, opened at the National. One inspiration was Isaiah Berlin's book of essays on Russian thinkers; another was Stoppard's abiding interest in the position of writers in totalitarian societies. Originally he planned a single play about the revolutionary thinker Alexander Herzen. But then he became absorbed in the life of the anarchist Michael Bakunin, who seemed an equally good subject. 'I began to think I'd need two plays. Then I thought, let's go for broke.' The resulting trilogy, which Trevor Nunn is soon to direct in the Olivier, has an ambitiously wide canvas.

Set in Russia, Paris and London and the Isle of Wight, it deals with the ferment of revolutionary ideas that swept through mid-nineteenth-century Europe. While the three plays – *Voyage*, *Shipwreck* and *Salvage* – centre on the turbulent lives of Herzen and Bakunin, Stoppard has also brought in other historical figures, including Karl Marx, the French socialist Louis Blanc and, most notably, the writer Ivan Turgenev.

Stoppard, now sixty-four, is disarmingly frank about the problems of tackling such a vast subject. 'I have to confess this was by far the most arduous thing I've done. I began to realise the brain couldn't cope in the way it used to do. I read all the sources twice before I started, but there was so much to keep in mind, if I left it alone for a few days I had to go back and read the material again. I didn't pace myself very well. In the end my notes took up much more paper than the plays themselves.'

A long-time admirer of Chekhov, he had been wanting to write a 'Russian play' for some time. In 1997 he worked on a version of *The Seagull* with Peter Hall. 'I've always felt very envious of Chekhov, the way nothing seems to be going on in his plays, and yet it's all intensely interesting and dramatic.' Gorky, in the shape of Trevor Nunn's 1999 production of *Summerfolk*, was another catalyst, notably for the first play of the trilogy, *Voyage*. 'As I sat in the Olivier I thought, I want to write one of these – with this actual set and these very people!'

Voyage is certainly more domestic in tone than Stoppard's earlier work: with its focus on family life on the Bakunin estate miles from Moscow, it could well have been called *Four Sisters*. The second and third plays are more overtly political: *Shipwreck* focuses on Herzen's activities during the failed 1848 revolution in France, while *Salvage* is set in his London home, a meeting place for exiled writers and activists, who argue violently about issues of the day such as the emancipation of the Russian serfs.

The trilogy's overall theme is the doomed quest for a utopian society. But, this being Stoppard, there are plenty of jokes, verbal misunderstandings and humorous exchanges in among the intense political debate – or what he describes as 'people shouting at each other'. He's clearly fascinated by the unpredictable Russian character. 'These people have very volatile natures, they turn on a sixpence, they're angry one moment and loving the next.' The plays highlight brilliantly the discrepancy between the characters' messy personal lives and their idealistic political pronouncements. 'To some extent I'm satirising them even while I'm admiring their ideas,' Stoppard says. 'I went into it seeing Herzen as a kind of hero, but in fact he was quite flawed, and I think that emerges.'

He admits to an empathy with Turgenev, the archetypal liberal: 'I always thought his role would be important, because I identify with him. I wanted to write about someone who was aware of his own moderation and is accused of essentially going neither left nor right. I feel that's rather true of myself.' Interestingly, he uses children – there are several in the trilogy – to up the emotional ante. 'You look for elements that will have a hold on the audience. When I was young I wasn't interested in that: I thought an audience should just follow an intellectual argument. I don't believe that any more, I don't think that alone can carry a play.'

Although the dialogue is necessarily his own creation, he's generally stuck closely to actual events and incidents, including the complicated, roller-coaster lives of Herzen and his friends. 'Just occasionally I've fudged the timescale, otherwise there would have been forty-seven scene changes,' he says. 'But I've not invented anything significant.' Paradoxically, his present membership of the National's Board turns out to be an inhibiting factor. 'I'm very conscious of how much things cost, so I sit there thinking, I'd better be careful here or we'll go over budget. But Bill Dudley, the designer, is a real tonic, he has such an appetite for challenges.

Do anything you like, he says; the more people turn up in all sorts of places, the better I like it.'

As usual Stoppard looks forward to attending rehearsals. 'Although I like the solitary side of writing – and it's quite hard to pull me out of it – I love rehearsals, because they create such a wonderful community. I love that feeling of looking at your work on the bench, of there first being the text, and then these people have to embody and express it. I'm not a director, but I'm quite good at technical things, I have quite good instincts. Of course, I have the advantage of having written the play.'

He's worked twice before with Trevor Nunn, on *Arcadia* at the National in 1993 and on *Every Good Boy Deserves Favour* in 1977. 'Trevor is the great examiner of texts, line by line,' he says. 'He's also relentless about not going too far too soon. With *Arcadia* I thought, will we ever start rehearsing? But the great thing was, when we did start we weren't constantly stopping to ask questions. We'd done all that.'

Unlike some playwrights, Stoppard is prepared to talk critically about a work before he's finished it. Even now he feels certain structural aspects of the three plays need finessing. 'I think Herzen's development as a political thinker ought to be made more coherent. I also feel I need to try and mix up more the domestic life and the editorials, to make the arguments grow more out of the characters' daily lives.' Making the inevitable cuts along the way has clearly been a painful process. 'I wanted to go through taking out all the bricks I could without the wall falling down. But then you think, "Wouldn't it be a pity not to save that one, and that one" – and you end up with a wall that makes a play too long.'

In their final shape the plays are, he believes, self-contained. 'I don't think it's necessary to see them in chronological order. I think that to learn more retroactively is sometimes more interesting.'

The Coast of Utopia opened in the Olivier in August 2002.

No whitewash over AIDS

Tony Kushner talks about his acclaimed new play *Angels in America*

The first part of Tony Kushner's extraordinary work *Angels in America* is already in the repertoire in America. Talking about the play on the eve of its opening at the National, the playwright stresses that he had not set out to write a documentary about AIDS. But neither had he wanted to pull punches. 'I really hate plays that whitewash the biological terrors that are part of the syndrome,' he says. 'I feel that's wrong and cowardly. If you take care of somebody with AIDS, it's very much about the horrible, horrible indignity the flesh has to suffer. It's about the body and the horrible poetry of disease, and I think it's important to represent that.'

At its centre the play deals both humorously and movingly with the lives of two gay men and the destructive effect that AIDS has on their relationship. As a gay man of thirty-five living in New York, Tony Kushner writes from experience, having already seen many of his friends die from AIDS. But this 'gay fantasia on national themes' is also about the Mormons, another of America's repressed minorities. Despite the Mormon Church's opposition to homosexuality, Kushner feels ambivalent towards the movement: 'I wanted to deal with a group that was ideologically problematic for me, but one which at the same time possesses many attractive features. I'm genuinely charmed by a lot of the Mormon theology – though of course I don't believe in it.'

The result is a sympathetic portrait of a young Mormon couple trying to get to grips with their gradual awareness of the husband's homosexuality. But Kushner's ability to empathise with people whose ideas may not be his is also in evidence in his depiction of Roy Cohn, Senator Joe McCarthy's notorious gay Jewish sidekick, and the man who helped send Ethel Rosenberg to the electric chair. In the play Cohn's quickfire wit, energy and larger-than-life villainy make him almost an attractive figure. Isn't this treading dangerous ground? 'I really enjoyed writing him,' Kushner confesses. 'But though he was a complete shit, probably one of the worst people that ever lived, in a weird way the play became for me a project of understanding someone like him.'

Cohn dies of AIDS, raising the question of how far the gay community should see him as one of theirs, as a victim as well as a moral reprobate. Kushner was appalled at many of the reactions to his death. 'As much as he was a disgusting person, the Left especially responded with a kind of homophobic contempt, and a real luxuriating in the details of his death, that I felt was completely reprehensible. So the play became one about forgiveness, which I think is an interesting political question.'

The National's production – there have been two in America – has taken him by surprise. 'It certainly doesn't look like what I had in mind,' he admitted. 'But Declan Donnellan is an amazing director, he's found another energy in the text, which is daring and exciting. It's also much more emotional: Declan has demanded of the actors that they recognise how high the stakes are for most of these people, and that they go for it and not be polite or correct, but be willing to be ugly.'

On the strength of the previews that he's seen, he's been delighted with the initial reaction. 'The National audiences have been terribly smart and attentive,' he says. 'I feel it's been easier to engage them than American audiences.' Although not many young people have seen it in America, he hopes that, despite the strong language and an explicit and brutal sexual encounter, the play will be seen by older teenagers at the National.

Angels in America opened in the Cottesloe in January 1992.

Innocent monster

Pam Gems captures the essence of a celebrated artist in *Stanley*

'Stanley Spencer is a genius, but people don't recognise the fact. Compared with him, people like Francis Bacon and Lucian Freud are mere journeymen.' Unwinding after a long day's rehearsal at the National, Pam Gems speaks passionately about her long-standing love of art, her likes and dislikes, and of the comparative neglect of the controversial painter whose complicated life provides the subject matter for her new play *Stanley*.

'Twenty years ago Stanley tended to be dismissed as a weirdo and a crank who painted people in funny shapes,' she says. 'You only admitted to liking his work apologetically, he was so unfashionable. But now that's changing.' Her play, with Antony Sher in the title role, centres on the celebrated painter's stormy relationships with his wife Hilda and his lover Patricia, and his doomed efforts to achieve the freedom in his private life that he found in his art.

Pam Gems is best known for writing biographical plays featuring female protagonists, the most notable examples being *Piaf, The Blue Angel, Camille* and *Queen Christina*. Even her best-known contemporary play, *Dusa, Fish, Stas and Vi*, has an all-female cast. 'When I came into theatre in my middle years I found there were very few roles for women,' she says. 'There was twice as much work for men, which meant that five years out of drama school a boy might have gained twice as much experience as his sister. I found that shocking.'

So why this sudden switch to a male central character? 'I didn't make a conscious decision to write about a man,' she explains. 'I just felt Stanley had been unfairly neglected and I wanted to celebrate a great painter.' She also clearly recognised the dramatic potential of this complex and infuriating artist's life. 'He was both an innocent and a monster: I love him deeply, but I also want to hit him. He tried to be totally truthful, but managed to destroy all his relationships.'

For Pam Gems there are practical advantages in writing plays based on real people. 'If you've only got two hours, and you're focusing on someone from history, you're starting with a world that people know, so in one sense you're already one act in.' She's used a wealth of source material to research Spencer's life: biographies, memoirs, art books and, of course, the paintings. 'But if you're writing a play rather than a documentary, you eventually simply throw away all your research and write from dramatic energy.'

Earlier I had watched her working with Antony Sher and director John Caird, the three of them meticulously exploring the subtext and fine-tuning the nuances of a particularly tricky scene between Spencer and Augustus John. She confesses to enjoying this kind of collaboration, but also warns of its dangers. 'At a certain point you have to stand back and let them cook it, so you can come in with a colder eye. Otherwise you become too much part of it, you just fall in love with everything that's being done, and find yourself unable to keep a critical distance.'

For Antony Sher's performance she is full of praise. 'Because he's played so many villains and creepy characters, I've always thought of him as a brilliant but cerebral actor. Then I worked with him on *Uncle Vanya* and he had me in tears. I hadn't realised until then that he could also be a very tender actor. That's when I thought of him for Stanley.'

Stanley opened in the Cottesloe in February 1996.

Double spies

Michael Frayn reflects on Germany, Willy Brandt and writing *Democracy*

I first went to Berlin in 1972 and was absolutely bowled over by it. It was the beginning of a lifelong fascination with Germany, during which I became intrigued by the complexity of German Federal politics. Writing a play about the four years of Willy Brandt's chancellorship seemed a good way of encapsulating it. It was a crucial period, which laid the foundations for ending the Cold War. And in spite of all the political difficulties, and his many weaknesses, I do think Brandt was a great man.

But when I looked further into those years I realised the story of his relationship with the spy Guillaume was more complex than I thought, with each of them spying on the other. Spying always interests me, because I'm fascinated by perception, by how people see the world in front of their eyes, and I suppose spying is an extreme case of perception, of people making sense of the world without revealing that they're watching and reporting on what they see.

I hope that audiences will find Guillaume a sympathetic character. Hegel once said, 'In a good play, everyone is right.' You can't follow that through one hundred per cent, but I certainly like to feel that every character in a play has a tenable viewpoint and is able to express it. I'm not interested in ones where there's a great hero or great villain, or where everyone is being denounced as a crook.

All the basic historical background in the play is as accurate as I can get it from the sources for the period, though I'm sure I've made mistakes. But the dialogue is completely invented. Even with Brandt's speeches about East Germany: he said these things, but they were more scattered and I've just pushed them together.

This is the seventh play of mine Michael Blakemore has directed. For me he's a great director, because he doesn't wish to impose some clever idea of his own, he wishes to do the play you've written. He's mainly worked on new plays, so he doesn't get the credit he deserves. A good director's contribution to a new play is enormous, but it's very tough on them, because no one outside has the faintest idea what it is, whereas with a classic everyone can see. If Hamlet comes in on roller skates, everyone knows that's the director's idea. But if I had Brandt going round on roller skates, who would know whose idea that was?

Once I've got a play as finished as possible, Michael and I go through it line by line, syllable by syllable. He makes me read it aloud to him – which is appalling, because I can't even hit the right stresses in my own lines. But it means we look at everything. He often asks stupid questions like, 'Why does he say that?' I start to say, 'Oh it's obvious' – and end up taking the line out, because it isn't. If *he* doesn't understand what's going on, the audience won't either.

Democracy opened in the Cottesloe in September 2003.

In search of ambiguity

Joe Penhall takes on the weapons industry in *Landscape with Weapon*

'Again it was one of those things that was under my nose. It was like found art and it just seemed an obvious subject for a play.'

After delving into psychiatry and mental illness in his wildly successful *Blue/Orange*, staged at the National in 2000, Joe Penhall has turned his attention to another hot but difficult subject. *Landscape with Weapon* is his coruscating study of a brilliant designer who resists the might of the weapons industry, with frightening consequences. Along the way he raises many very human as well as political questions.

'To some extent I use plays as a forum for working out arguments in my head, or those I've had with other people,' he says. 'Those in *Landscape* are ones that a lot of people have had, for example about ownership of an idea, and the devastation of having your idea traduced. I think anyone working in a creative field can relate to that.'

Though his plays are clearly well researched, they don't involve endless trips to the British Library. 'I find stories the same way a journalist would – I talk to people and get a lead, and then go sniffing for a little more. I'll ask friends or people I meet in bars or at parties – there's no rigid orthodoxy,' he explains. 'But it's usually something they or I have first-hand experience of.' *Blue/Orange* came about through a friend working with mentally ill people in San Francisco. 'I helped him out for a couple of weeks. One of his guys was a black man, whose delusions were either that he was white, or a woman. He was fascinating and irrepressible, so I started writing down what he said, and it just leapt off the page.'

For his new play he has drawn on conversations with a friend who is a weapons designer, who then suggested other areas he could dig around in. He tracked down a robot expert, who took him to a robot convention. And in New York he met an agent for Homeland Security. 'We talked and hung out, and I thought wow, this guy's a spy and I really like him. So he informed one of the characters a bit. But none of them are photocopies of the guys I met.'

Born in London but brought up in Australia, where he went to art school, Penhall worked as chief reporter on a London local paper before his first play *Some Voices* was accepted by the Royal Court in 1994 and subsequently staged around the world. He's found that journalistic experience invaluable. 'It was a wonderful portal into society, because I got sent everywhere – to the police station, the town hall, the fire station. That gave me an insight into the machinations of the community and provided a great informal education. It also taught me a lot as a writer. So I know how to zero in on a story and log it, how to separate the wheat from the chaff, how to seek out different points of view.'

He is, though, scornful of what he calls 'journalistic' plays: 'I really resent those preachy, topical plays that purport to tell us what's going on, but are just recycling what we can read in the papers. I think they insult the intelligence of the audience. The whole point of the theatre is to provide something completely original that could only come from the theatre and nowhere else.'

He admits that *Landscape with Weapon* has given him a different challenge from *Blue/Orange*. 'There's no right side to take in the argument about what to do with the mentally ill; it's one of those terrible human conundrums. But when it comes to a play about weapons, people have pretty much made up their minds. So it's much harder to be ambiguous about it.'

Landscape with Weapon opened in the Cottesloe in April 2007.

A question of forgiving

Bryony Lavery on the emotional impetus behind *Frozen,* her play about a serial paedophile killer

Bryony Lavery remembers a time when she dreamed of hijacking the National Theatre. 'We used to have meetings about the problems facing women playwrights and directors. My plan was that we should break in, take over the National and say, "Now it's the women's turn!"'

These days there's no need for any breaking and entering; she's stormed the building through merit, not violence. This summer she became one of the few playwrights to have two plays – *Frozen* and *Illyria* – staged at the National in the same month. It's a thrilling and much-deserved achievement for someone who has been working non-stop for more than a quarter of a century, writing over forty plays, pantomimes and cabarets, both for children and adults.

'People kept saying you ought to be pleased to be at the National, but I just paid it lip service,' she says. 'Then during rehearsals for *Frozen* I thought, this is the National Theatre of my country! I suddenly realised what it meant, and felt a burst of nationalistic pride. It was quite extraordinary.' Media coverage prompted by the play, which has just finished a successful run in the Cottesloe, has suggested she's been underrated as a playwright. She herself sees the matter differently. 'The reason a lot of people haven't heard of me is because I've been doing plays in places like Ludlow Castle,' she says. 'It's easier to get to the Court and the National.'

Now fifty-four, she wrote her first play at school – secretly, in Latin. 'It wasn't performed, just sniggered at.' At home she was already writing in her head. 'My kid sister and I weren't allowed to have television, so we used to invent incredibly complex stories.' At college, encouraged by an exceptional teacher and former actor ('He was a complete guru to me'), she wrote three plays, then taught in various London schools ('I was a very theatrical teacher') and ran a theatre company, before getting her first commission and discovering she could earn a living from playwriting.

There's a simple explanation as to why she's so prolific. 'I really enjoy writing and find it incredibly interesting; I also like to work on two or three plays at a time. But I've also learnt to push things. I treat myself as the workforce: if she's feeling a bit stodgy I give her the day off; if she isn't working well on one play, I say go and work in another department for a bit.'

Most of her early work and middle plays are comedies; *Her Aching Heart*, for example, was a hilarious parody of the world of romantic fiction à la Georgette Heyer. But more recently her work has become darker. 'For the last four or five years I've felt the need to tackle subjects that really frighten me,' she explains. 'I think I've grown up in various areas. Because I've had some hard knocks, especially with both my parents dying, I somehow feel I've earned the right to tackle serious subjects.'

The overt subject of *Frozen* could hardly be more serious. The play deals with the complex relationship between a serial paedophile killer and the mother of one of his victims, who eventually forgives him for ending her daughter's life. Yet while the story is based on those of several real-life child murderers, including Fred West, at a deeper level it owes its emotional impetus to the death of Bryony Lavery's mother. 'She went into hospital for a simple operation, which went wrong because of a tyro surgeon. That required an enormous amount of forgiveness,' she recalls.

Many people assumed that *A Wedding Story*, her play about Alzheimer's, acclaimed two years ago at the Birmingham Rep, was based on personal experience. But neither of her parents had the disease. 'In a sense I think it was a way of reclaiming a parent, of saying goodbye,' she says. 'I always have to go off-centre to imagine, because I'm a fiction writer, not a chronicler of my life.'

Her second play recently at the National, *Illyria*, prompted by the war in Bosnia, was created for schools and youth groups taking part in the InterNational Connections project. Written in typically poetic language, it's a powerful and savage piece that deals with the horrors of civil war as seen by a foreign correspondent. 'I think young people need to take on difficult subjects; they have experiences they can bring to a play like this,' she says. Like her other 'serious' plays, *Illyria* is not short of humour. 'It's one of the few OK weapons, isn't it,' she suggests. 'You can wound with humour, but you can also protect, and defuse serious situations. I've never been through a dreadful experience without at some point having a really good laugh at something ludicrous.'

Frozen opened in the Cottesloe in July 2002.

Complex matters

In *The Talking Cure* Christopher Hampton untangles the difficult relationship between Freud and Jung

Christopher Hampton takes a characteristically detached view of Freudian psychoanalysis. 'I've never been really convinced by all the paraphernalia, but I do think it was one of the great imaginative ventures of the twentieth century.'

Although he has never undergone analysis himself, he became absorbed by Freud's ideas many years ago. Then in the 1980s he heard about Sabina Spielrein, a young Russian patient of Jung whose papers had been found in a suitcase in Geneva. 'Nobody quite knew what it was, but clearly there was a very interesting dynamic between her and Jung, and she had obviously been an element in the relationship between him and Freud, and in their break-up. But like a lot of subjects that catch your fancy, I couldn't figure out how to do it.'

In the 1990s more papers, including diaries and letters, became available, and it became clear that Jung and Spielrein had an affair. By now Hampton was hooked: he got hold of the original notes of her case, then wrote a screenplay that had Spielrein at its centre. She seemed a strong subject: an impressive figure in her own right, she went on to become an analyst, train Jean Piaget in Geneva and a whole generation of analysts in Russia, before being killed by the Nazis during the war.

But the screenplay didn't work out. 'I still didn't seem to have landed on the right runway,' Hampton recalls. 'Eventually it came to me with a resounding clang that as a play it should really be centred on Jung, as he was the key figure between Freud and Sabina.' In the end, after a typically lengthy period of gestation, the play 'burst out in ten days', in a very different shape from the screenplay.

As with his play *Total Eclipse*, which dealt with the tortured friendship between the poets Rimbaud and Verlaine, he has stuck closely to the historical facts, with only minor fiddling with the chronology. 'I'm firmly of the belief that what happens in real life is much more interesting than anything you could make up,' he says. 'You obviously have to invent tones of voice and interpretations of people's motives. But generally with my historical plays I gather all the main facts, then fill in the gaps.'

Researching the lives of Freud, the father of psychoanalysis, and Jung, at one time seen as his heir, has brought its surprises. 'It comes as a bit of a shock with these intellectual giants to find out how human they were; for example, how petty Freud was, or how badly Jung behaved at certain times. But it's also reassuring, it brings them into our world rather than leaving them on Parnassus, where such figures tend to get put without due consideration that they were just as bewildered as the rest of us.'

He's particularly pleased to have Ralph Fiennes on board for the production, since he wrote Jung with him in mind. 'I often write with actors' voices in my head: they give you a fixed image with which to anchor yourself. Even if you can't get those ones, which is what usually happens, they've served a purpose.' He feels Fiennes is one of the few actors who can play an intellectual character convincingly. 'He has a thoughtful quality, and a candour and charisma about him that is very apt for Jung, who was very open and outgoing, at least in his work, whereas Freud was rather guarded and suspicious, and wounded by all the battles.'

The clash between, loosely speaking, a classicist and a romantic is familiar territory for Hampton: he himself likens it to the encounter between Brecht and Horváth that he imagined in his play *Tales from Hollywood*. 'I never knew which side to come down on, so it's obviously very fruitful ground for me,' he suggests. 'It's like examining the difference between radicals and liberals, which is often more bitter than between radicals and conservatives. It's interesting paddling in those waters.'

As with his earlier plays, a lot of the story is embedded in the subtext, in what his characters are *not* saying. 'The scenes between Freud and Jung appear to be about intellectual matters, but there are all kinds of things seething below the surface. Likewise with Jung and Sabina: what is said between them is only about a tenth of what's going on.' This is why he's delighted to have Howard Davies as his director. 'Howard is very good at uncovering what's beneath the words. He's incomparably good on emotional quagmires, he knows how to present them in a very palpable way.'

This is Hampton's first original play since the semi-autobiographical *White Chameleon*, staged at the National in 1991. In recent years he's been heavily involved with films, both as writer and director; even now he's having to miss certain rehearsals in order to edit his latest screen venture, *Imagining Argentina*, about the people who disappeared in that country. 'But I love the theatre and really enjoy rehearsals, so I'm very pleased to be back.'

The Talking Cure opened in the Cottesloe in January 2003.

Naturalistic and surreal

Martin McDonagh fills in the background to *The Cripple of Inishmaan*

A play with a teenage crippled orphan as its hero seems an unlikely candidate for a black comedy, but that's precisely what twenty-six-year-old Martin McDonagh has created with his new play *The Cripple of Inishmaan*, which has just opened in the Cottesloe under the direction of Nicholas Hytner.

Set in 1934 on one of the three Aran Islands off the west coast of Ireland, it's a richly humorous story, played out by an engaging bunch of Irish characters that never descend into stereotypes. Centring on the arrival on a neighbouring island of the Hollywood director Robert Flaherty to film his documentary *Man of Aran*, it tells the tale of seventeen-year-old Billy's determined efforts to land a part in the film and become a movie star. Somehow it manages to be simultaneously naturalistic and surreal, violent and gentle, bawdy and poignant.

So how did McDonagh manage to avoid sentimentalising Billy's disability? 'I like my characters and I want them to be true,' he says. 'If you begin from that standpoint, then in writing comedy you don't fall into that trap.' His play is part of a planned trilogy, one for each of the Aran Islands. 'I think a trilogy makes a story seem more grand,' he says. *The Cripple of Inishmaan*, his second play, marks his debut at the National. It follows the success of *The Beauty Queen of Leenane*, which was highly praised when it was staged last year at the Royal Court, and won him the 1996 George Devine Award for Most Promising Playwright.

Though his parents are Irish – his father hails from Galway, his mother from Sligo – he himself was born, bred and schooled in England. He claims his reason for taking up writing was a prosaic one: 'It was lack of money that got me started.' At sixteen he began with screenplays, moving on to short 'film stories', then radio plays. He sent no less than twenty-two to the BBC, which rejected all of them. 'After a while I think they stopped reading them, but doing them helped me to develop the skill of writing dialogue,' he says. Perhaps disingenuously, he claims not to think much about the craft or mechanics of writing, arguing that anyone can write a play if they set their mind to it. But he clearly likes to get a script as polished as possible before showing it to others: the draft of *The Cripple of Inishmaan* that he delivered to the National needed only minor amendments during rehearsal.

As the recipient of the Pearson Television Theatre Writers' Scheme award he was given £5,000, which enabled him to put aside time to get the play written. 'That was the best kind of support a writer can get,' he says. He was also offered a week-long workshop with a group of actors in the National's Studio, and a performance of his play in front of an invited audience. 'It resulted in a bit of tinkering, especially with the jokes,' he recalls. Sitting in on rehearsals was both an enjoyable and valuable experience. 'It's important for the writer to be able to explain or clarify. Of course the actors and director are free to accept or reject what you come up with.'

The Cripple of Inishmaan opened in the Cottesloe in January 1997.

A dream quality

Rebecca Lenkiewicz on making her debut at the National with *The Night Season*

To have only your second play staged at the National would be any playwright's dream. When Rebecca Lenkiewicz heard that *The Night Season* was to join the Cottesloe repertoire she could hardly believe her good fortune. 'I was euphoric, I was walking on air, it seemed completely unreal.'

But nine months later, as we talk at the National halfway through rehearsals, it's clear that some less joyful emotions are mingling with her delight. 'I do sometimes have this impulse to run away,' she confesses. 'It's wonderful having the play being done here, but there's also a kind of embarrassment, an occasional feeling that it's the emperor's new clothes. I see a lot of new plays and I'm constantly making comparisons. Some days I wonder why the National are doing mine, on other days I think it reads well. But there's definitely a fear.'

This mixture of anxiety and self-deprecation is not unknown among playwrights as they approach the moment when their work will be exposed to the outside world. But in Rebecca Lenkiewicz's case it seems in complete contrast to the wit, exuberance and romanticism of *The Night Season*.

Though it's not a portrait of her own family, she admits she has drawn to some extent on her own background. Born and brought up in Plymouth, she's the third in a tightly knit family of three brothers and two sisters. 'My sister and I grew up with a deep sense of romance, and falling in love with strangers,' she remembers. 'We loved films, we loved Hollywood musicals, we loved that whole other world, and I think that's reflected in many of the images and themes in the play.'

Her first idea was to write about the poet W. B. Yeats and his unrequited love for the beautiful, fiery Irish nationalist Maud Gonne. But the plan soon underwent a sea change. 'I love Yeats' poetry and I was fascinated by his obsession with Maud Gonne; it was like the old idea of the knight, sick with love and melancholia. But then I decided I wanted to write something modern as well. At first I thought I could weave together two parallel relationships, but the modern voices took over in my head, so Yeats had to go.'

Though she has some Irish blood in her background and has spent time in Ireland, she's never actually lived there. Yet the modern voices that came into her head were always distinctly Irish. 'More than anything else I wanted to write something lyrical,' she says. 'I think the Irish voice can carry that off, whereas the English voice can just sound flowery. I wanted language that could fly, and I do think it's easier to get that with the Irish, without it sounding fey – which of course is a danger.'

She showed early drafts to actor and playwright Jack Shepherd, with whom she'd worked several times. 'I'm fascinated by dreams, and at that stage it was more like a dream play and quite surreal. Jack was very supportive, but said that the play might last six hours if it was to make sense within a dream structure. Although it's now a realistic play, I hope it still has a kind of dream quality.'

A rehearsed reading at the Actors' Centre gave her further food for thought. 'It was brilliant to hear it spoken and very valuable,' she recalls. 'I realised there was too much subtext floating around and not enough action. It was too vague; I could see it needed sharpening up.' After a major rewrite she sent it to the National's associate director Howard Davies, with whom she had worked as an actress on Bulgakov's *Flight*. He was clear at once that the National should stage it.

One of Rebecca Lenkiewicz's sternest critics is her father Peter Quint, a poet, novelist and playwright. 'His plays have been a huge influence on me, as has his love of words,' she says. 'I respect his opinion completely, he's a brilliant and very specific critic, and an amazing writer.' She makes it clear, though, that Patrick Kennedy, the father in the play, is not based on him, but is an amalgam of several people she knows. Nor is the feisty, romantic grandmother drawn from life – although she does have one reference that's clearly based on family history. The story goes that her great-grandmother was living in an old people's home on the day Prince Philip paid a visit. As he tried to shake her hand she said: 'Fuck off! Who do you think I am, a fucking monkey?'

With director Lucy Bailey she recently visited Sligo for the first time. 'We both wanted to check that the play could have happened there, and it did feel right.' In their search for the kind of backwater the Kennedy family might have lived in, they eventually came across one house that seemed to fit the bill. 'This old woman came to the door and told us she'd lived there for ninety years, which seemed like a good omen.'

Though *The Night Season* is her second play, it's the first she's written with a production consciously in mind. Her first piece, *Soho – A Tale of Table Dancers*, was, she says, 'a bit of a fluke, it was just a flood of words, almost subconscious. It was based on my experiences working at a table-dancing club. I was unhappy at the time, but it came out as a comedy and that was quite therapeutic. Then I just put it away in a drawer.' Later she took it out again and reworked it for the RSC Fringe at the 2000 Edinburgh Festival, where it won a Fringe First and subsequently opened London's Arcola Theatre.

After writing the first version of *Soho* she trained at Central and pursued an acting career. Acting, she says, has hugely informed her writing. 'As an actress I've become very aware of text, of what works and what doesn't. It's made me keen, too, to make sure everyone has a decent part. Also I tend to speak the lines out loud while I'm writing. I'm always having conversations with the characters, even when I'm riding my bike.'

Though she loves acting, she doesn't seem too concerned that it's recently had to take a back seat. 'I've had some lovely parts and ideally I'd like to continue with both careers. But if I had to choose I would definitely write. Writing makes me feel more alive, whereas acting is often more limited. With writing all you need is ideas and a pen, but with acting you need a company.'

Her writing career certainly seems to be developing nicely. She's in the middle of a year's attachment at the Soho Theatre, who have commissioned her next stage play, and she's just finishing her first radio play, about a 1950s teacher who was once a suffragette. She's refreshingly candid about this experience. 'I thought a forty-five-minute play would just roll off the wrist, but it didn't. With radio I imagined it would just be a matter of dialogue, you just had to make the story happen, with no worries about staging. But I found it much harder than I thought I would to make the story alive.'

With far fewer acting roles for women than men, she reckons life is much tougher for an actress than it is for a female playwright. 'I think there's equality now for writers; gender doesn't affect whether a play is accepted or not. Theatres are just after good, varied work, whoever it's from.'

The Night Season opened in the Cottesloe in August 2004.

Shocking facts and verbatim theatre

David Hare discusses his provocative documentary play *The Permanent Way*

When Max Stafford-Clark suggested he might write a play about the railways, David Hare admits he thought the subject a bit nerdish. 'But the minute I began looking into it I was riveted. Like everybody else I thought I knew the story, but I didn't. British Rail, whatever its inadequacies, functioned. Now we have a system that doesn't. And when I investigated how and why the privatisation decision had been taken, I was shocked to discover that not a single person would now defend it.'

The Permanent Way, which has already received rave reviews on its pre-National tour, is a hard-hitting documentary play based heavily on the direct testimony of a cross-section of witnesses, ranging from those involved in making the critical decision, to others who survived or were bereaved by the subsequent crashes. Directed by Max Stafford-Clark, it grew out of a workshop at the National's Studio, during which Hare wrote a short play, which the actors performed at the end. He then did more research, talked to more people and filled the play out. The actors did many of the interviews, then improvised their situation for Hare after they'd met the people involved. 'Six of the workshop company are in the final play and that's helped immensely,' Hare says. 'The fact that they know the people has given their characterisation greater depth.'

One of his main themes is the difference between the emotional attitude of the survivors and that of the bereaved. 'Generally if you are a survivor it's an experience you want to put behind you. The bereaved, on the other hand, want to understand why a member of their family had to die, so they put it behind them less easily, and many don't want to do so at all. So, as one character says, they're not the hysterical bereaved, but the informed bereaved. I think politicians have been surprised to discover how powerfully informed they are.'

The play also addresses the question of corporate manslaughter. But here Hare has had to be cautious, since the result of the police investigation into the Potter's Bar crash is still awaited, and there are prosecutions pending over Hatfield and Ladbroke Grove. 'Nothing would distress me more than if I made a mistake that endangered any prosecution, so the play has been thoroughly vetted by lawyers. There's a lot more I'd love to be able to put in, but I can't. I have to be fantastically careful.'

Some parts of his script are taken verbatim from the interviews. 'There's an extraordinary speech by a woman who lost her son in the Southall crash. When I read it back, it was like reading D. H. Lawrence; it was unimprovable.' With other parts he has acted as playwright rather than journalist. 'I've reorganised some of the material to try to get at the essence of what people were trying to say.' He's been careful not to misuse the material he's been offered. 'People who've been victims or suffered because of the crashes have read the play, and commented on the way they're presented. They've asked me to put things in or take things out, and I absolutely have to respect their wishes. The last thing you want to do is to cause hurt to anybody who's already been hurt.'

As a playwright with a penchant for documentary theatre and plays about politics, he believes there's a great thirst for this type of theatre. 'I've always believed that people want to understand their own history, they want to see it laid out in some kind of epic form. Unfortunately there's always been a shortage of individuals in the theatre willing to provide it. This mystifies me, because in real life people are fascinated by the subject.'

The Permanent Way opened in the Cottesloe in January 2004.

Playhouse creatures

April De Angelis on David Garrick, Oliver Goldsmith and *A Laughing Matter*

Theatre life is clearly a compelling subject for April De Angelis. Five years ago she wrote *Playhouse Creatures*, a witty, bawdy and poignant play featuring Nell Gwyn, Thomas Otway, Mrs Betterton and the Earl of Rochester. Now she's back behind the historical stage with *A Laughing Matter*, a rumbustious and moving work with a cast of characters headed by David Garrick, Peg Woffington, Dr Johnson and Oliver Goldsmith.

Her play centres on Garrick's refusal as actor-manager of Drury Lane to stage Goldsmith's *She Stoops to Conquer*. 'It was a gift to Garrick, the best play written for fifty years,' she says. 'I wanted to find out why he made that decision.' The result of her enquiry, an entertaining story about the public and private life of the greatest actor of his age, will shortly alternate in the Lyttelton with Goldsmith's eternally delightful comedy.

The idea of commissioning a new play linked to a classic, and staging them together, came from Max Stafford-Clark, artistic director of Out of Joint. He had already done this successfully with Timberlake Wertenbaker – first with *Our Country's Good* and Farquhar's *The Recruiting Officer*, then with *Break of Day* and Chekhov's *Three Sisters*. But the idea is not a new one for April De Angelis: in 1997 Dominic Dromgoole staged her *Playhouse Creatures* at the Old Vic alongside Vanbrugh's *The Provok'd Wife*, which in turn featured in her play.

The new commission has involved her in reading sheaves of eighteenth-century plays. 'We thought we might discover a forgotten play; many women were writing them, which was exciting,' she recalls. 'But they were really disappointing, very long-winded and sentimental. So it came to a choice between Goldsmith and Sheridan, who were writing against the sentimental tradition.'

Since she started writing plays thirteen years ago, her output has been impressively varied; she seems equally at home with settings ancient and modern. Vigorous, fresh, full of robust humour, her work ranges from the poetic historical fantasy *Ironmistress* (for the ReSisters Theatre Company) to the haunting, enigmatic *Hush* (for the Royal Court), from her reminiscence-based *The Warwickshire Testimony* (for the RSC) to her hard-hitting look at feminism, *The Positive Hour* (for Out of Joint). She has also written *Soft Vengeance* for Graeae Theatre Company, the opera *Flight* with Jonathan Dove for Glyndebourne, and plays for radio.

Despite years of steady success and being in demand, the fact that she has nearly always worked to commission some-times worries her. 'Theatres or theatre companies have always offered me subjects and I don't know if that's good or bad,' she says. 'I haven't found a distinctive approach and I wonder if that's a fault.' In fact, though *The Positive Hour* was commissioned by Max Stafford-Clark, the choice of subject in this case was her own.

'I was trying to find a way of thinking about ideologies. I've been in loads of different women's groups: a women students' group at university, a women's therapy group, all-women households; I grew up in that sort of culture. They're a brilliant idea, but they're as flawed as anything else, and when they get into the wrong hands they can become very double-edged and destructive.' Though she called herself a feminist playwright when she started out, she would now avoid the label. 'I think that sensibility will be with me for the whole of my life, but to me people are just writers who have certain beliefs.'

Now a mother with a nine-year-old daughter, she thinks it's become easier for women writers to make the grade. 'When I was starting out I remember a female literary manager claiming there was something in women's make-up that made them unable to write plays. Nowadays people don't want to put up any barriers to new writing. A lot of that comes down to Caryl Churchill: being a great writer, she knocked down people's prejudices. Of course, there still aren't as many plays staged by women writers as there are by men, but that's not just to do with theatre: it's very hard to write with a young child running around.'

She's disarmingly frank about the difficulties of sustaining a momentum as a playwright. 'It gets harder as you go on, because you become more aware. When you start you've got nothing to lose, but when you're a mature adult you're really expected to deliver the goods. It's no longer good enough just to say, I want to express myself. Now it's got to be, What are you saying? Why are you saying it? Are you good enough to say it?'

She acknowledges her debt to Max Stafford-Clark while she's been writing *A Laughing Matter*. 'He's been really tenacious with me, I think I might have given up otherwise. Each time you give him a draft he finds something new and good in it. He's fantastically good with scripts: once he's commissioned your play he'll work on it with you until it's right.'

A Laughing Matter opened in the Lyttelton in September 2002.

A new generation

Kwame Kwei-Armah reveals the nature and origins of *Fix Up*

I was pleased and honoured that my first play, *Elmina's Kitchen*, had such an impact at the National, that it reached out to and drew in a different kind of audience. I think this has helped to contribute to the notion that Britain is really dealing with inclusiveness across the board, that artistically all languages and all communities are valid in the arena of cultural analysis. The play's success validated Nicholas Hytner's bold decision to put it on in such an environment.

I had hoped it would be a catalyst for a debate about the problem of a black underclass. I think to a great extent it has achieved that, both within the black community and nationally. It's on university syllabuses, people are studying it, I'm asked into schools to talk about it, and I've been invited on to government round tables on the subject. So there have been many positive outcomes.

There are still, of course, huge problems. We're looking at one in four black men unemployed under the age of twenty-four, and that's a depression. We're looking at fewer black young men in universities than in custodial institutions. We're looking at young black boys, particularly Caribbean boys, not doing terribly well at school, leaving with very low qualifications, not going into the system, and having to create their own environments and cultural rules in order to survive. So for me the burning issue is the failure of the education system.

However, what we must always applaud is the movement forward, in terms of integration and equality. In many respects it's a very different place from when I was growing up. Thirty years ago it was considered acceptable to call me 'sambo, nigger, rubber lips', to tell me to go back to the jungle – and if you talked about it you were seen as having a chip on your shoulder. Now that is no longer acceptable language and that's a positive change. Our country has strived towards a notion of equality in ways that maybe only America and the new South Africa have done.

Elmina's Kitchen was partly inspired by my hearing August Wilson give a speech during a Black History Month in America, when he spoke about the Afro-American experience throughout the twentieth century. That solidified and crystallised certain ideas in my mind, and made me realise I wanted to write about the black British experience, to celebrate the pioneering generation, and to look at the woes and the joys of being black British at this time.

Fix Up came from various sources. At first I thought I'd write a trilogy of *Elmina*. Then I decided to write a play for each of the black institutions – a restaurant, a bookstore, a church. Then I saw Patrick Marber's play *After Miss Julie*, which I loved, and which prompted me to think I should do an adaptation of it, but make the woman West Indian. I considered setting it in 1950s Grenada or Trinidad, but then thought, where better to set it thematically than in a shop in London that deals with black history, with the liberation one can get when one understands one's past? Those were the seeds from which I created the *Fix Up* bookstore, and a mixed-race daughter who turns the world of her newly found father upside down.

I'm fascinated with black history, with the institution of slavery, with the period of enslavement, and I've always wanted to write a play about it. But in a way we've become a little jaded with plays about slavery, we somehow feel that because we saw *Roots* on television in the 1970s we've got the measure of it. However, the multiplicity of narratives about Jewish existence and the Holocaust shows me that you can attack history from several thousand different angles, that you can still make it interesting if you can tap into the human experience of it.

With playwriting, as with any narrative, you have to have something to say. I wanted to talk about the mixed-race generation that's coming up, that's about to ask for a voice of its own. I wanted to talk about the pain of living in the past and living now, and having to reinvent yourself. I wanted to talk about black history, about the rich tradition of black literature, of the intellectual thought and philosophy and theology that we have. But I also wanted to explore the human aspect of fathers and daughters, of the different generations, of reparations for past sins.

While I was writing the play the National gave it a workshop in their Studio, with the Hollywood actor Delroy Lindo coming over to take part. For writers to have this resource is a phenomenal asset. It shows the National takes your art seriously, providing a space where you can experiment, throw things around and release the best that you have within you. I only wish all writers could have access to such a wonderful facility.

Fix Up opened in the Cottesloe in December 2004.

Whose bomb was it anyway?

Michael Frayn reflects on the scientific and other matters he explores in *Copenhagen*

They were two of the greatest physicists of the twentieth century. They were also close friends and professional colleagues. During the 1939–1945 war they became deeply involved in attempts to build a nuclear bomb. There was one problem: they were working for opposite sides in the conflict.

Michael Frayn's new play *Copenhagen* explores the complex relationship between the Danish physicist Niels Bohr and his German counterpart Werner Heisenberg. In it he looks at the dilemmas facing scientists working to perfect weapons of mass destruction, and in particular at that of Heisenberg, who was opposed to the Nazi regime, but headed their nuclear research programme. 'The Germans didn't get anywhere near making a nuclear bomb,' Frayn explains. 'But the question is, was this because Heisenberg, who opposed the Nazis, was deliberately dragging his feet because of reluctance to arm Hitler with the bomb? Or were they just working on the wrong lines? There's evidence for both explanations.'

Talking just before rehearsals begin, he makes it clear that he's aimed for historical accuracy where possible. 'The meeting of the two men in 1941 in Copenhagen is a fact, but almost everything else is a matter of conjecture and dispute,' he says. 'So then it's a question of trying to get inside the characters' heads and see the world as they saw it.' In *Copenhagen* he does this by moving the action back and forwards in time, with the two men trying to reconstruct their crucial wartime encounter, but failing to agree on the simplest details or each other's motives. Only Bohr's wife Margarethe, the voice of common sense unversed in science, is able to cut through to what really happened. She also acts as a useful sounding board for the men's scientific ideas, forcing them to make them comprehensible to her and therefore to the audience.

Although he's a successful novelist as well as a playwright –

he's just finished another novel while waiting for the National to find a slot for *Copenhagen* – Frayn always felt the Bohr–Heisenberg story would work most effectively as a play. 'In a novel you have direct access to the thinking of the author, whereas on stage the audience has to judge the characters' motives and behaviour from the outside, as in life,' he observes. 'And as *Copenhagen* is about the difficulties we have knowing other people's intentions, as well as our own, theatre seemed to me to be the best medium.'

Despite a certain amount of bandying around of scientific ideas in the play, the dialogue manages to be accessible to a non-scientific audience. But the playwright has made sure he's got his facts right by having had the script checked by two scientists, one of them a nuclear physicist. 'Before I began I understood one or two of the basic scientific ideas, but I had to do a great deal of homework,' he admits. 'Even now I wouldn't say I understand very much of it and certainly not the mathematics. But I think the conceptual issues can be expressed and understood.'

He acknowledges the valuable help he's had from director Michael Blakemore. 'Directors often work with the writer of a new play to get the text right, but rarely get credit for doing so. Michael was very good at telling me what he didn't understand and as a result I've simplified it a bit.' It remains a challenging play, and all the more absorbing for concentrating on essentially human and personal questions, rather than turning the exercise into a heavy-handed debate about the moral responsibility of science.

'What I'm finally interested in is the way human beings work,' Frayn says. 'To what extent is there some random, unexaminable element in part of our behaviour over which we have no control? Because the whole possibility of moral responsibility depends on us having control of our actions.'

Copenhagen opened in the Cottesloe in May 1998.

Net effect

Nick Darke on *The Riot,* his version of a dramatic
moment in Cornish history

Like most of my plays, *The Riot* is set in Cornwall, because
that's where I come from. My family was originally a seafaring
one, which settled in Cornwall four generations ago. I was
brought up in the house where I now live. The Cornish
element in my work is very strong, because those are and have
been the voices around me. It's a very distinctive dialect, and
the rhythms of speech I hear when I'm writing dialogue tend to
be those I remember from childhood.

I think that applies to a lot of writers: there's a time when
your ear is particularly attuned to the language around you.
But I had to move away from Cornwall in order to make it as
a playwright. It was only after I'd achieved a certain status that
I felt able to move back. And for the first couple of years it was
fairly rough going. It felt like starting all over again. What
helped was having my plays produced by Kneehigh Theatre,
which is based in Cornwall – though I don't write my plays for
them, or use them to develop a script. But there are now actors
who were born and raised in Cornwall, or who have lived there
all their lives and have a knowledge and understanding of the
place. Now we know each other so well, there's a great
company feeling.

I've worked as an actor and I write as an actor: my plays
aren't works of literature, they're like a set of architect's plans,
from which the director as builder works. A good builder
constantly refers to the architect, he doesn't put his own
interpretation on the plans. And the architect is constantly
saying, 'Change the colour of that brick', or 'The texture of
that concrete is wrong'. That's exactly what I've been doing
with *The Riot.*

I'm a fisherman myself and a lot of my plays have been about
fishing folk. But I can't write documentary plays; I have to have
room to create my own world. If I had to write something
about a specific incident and just stick to the facts, my

strengths as a writer wouldn't come through. What happens in *The Riot* is nothing like what actually took place – but also it is. All these things did happen, though not in a single day as they do in the play. They've been filtered through my own prism, allowing me to use my own voice, to create my own colour, texture and richness.

A riot occurred in the port of Newlyn in May 1896. Mackerel fishermen, who were staunch Methodists and didn't go to sea on the Sabbath, objected to visiting boats from Lowestoft working on Sunday, landing their fish on Monday and lowering prices for the rest of the week. A thousand fishermen gathered on the quay at dawn. The East Coast men, who were outnumbered and to some degree sympathetic to Sunday Observance, sat and watched as their complete catch was tipped into the harbour. The rest of the Lowestoft fleet, loaded with mackerel and ready to land, were diverted to Penzance. That's when the trouble started. Newlyn and Penzance, being close neighbours, were deadly enemies. Newlyn fishermen marched on Penzance to halt the landings and were met with a huge crowd spoiling for a fight. The army was sent for, a battalion arrived and a battleship was moored in Mount's Bay.

I've always wanted to write a play about that riot, because it has such a wonderful theatrical curve. It starts quietly with the conspiracy, things go to plan at first, then they start to get out of control, then pockets of violence erupt, then there's the huge confrontation and finally the aftermath. So I chose the subject for theatrical rather than political reasons.

But there's no point in plundering the past unless you intend to illuminate the present. And I could see so many parallels in the Newlyn riot with our own time. It was the end of the century, so there were hopes and fears like we have. The fishing industry was in crisis, as it is now. And there was emigration from Cornwall, as there is now.

The Riot opened in the Cottesloe in February 1999.

Themes and images

Charlotte Jones reveals what inspired her to write *Humble Boy*

My plays often begin with an image. For *In Flame* the first one was of the old woman tap-dancing at the moment when she died. During the gestation period of *Humble Boy* I had this image of a man at the top of a hive, in a bee-keeping suit that looked like a space suit, about to jump, and then he dies.

I'd also been thinking about male depression and the very high suicide rate among young men. A friend from Oxford, a bit of a golden boy with a top first in English, had developed schizophrenia, and had gone back to live at home and work in a charity shop. I was really haunted by his story, because he was so aware of all that he'd lost.

I wanted to write a play set in an English country garden, though I'm not quite sure why. I had this image of a golden boy – who became Felix Humble – stumbling about in a garden with bees in it. I'd also been interested in mother–son relationships for a long time, and the more I thought about Felix's mother, the more it suggested *Hamlet*. All these themes and images became connected in my head.

I thought, I can either ignore the *Hamlet* idea or embrace it. I chose to embrace it. And that was brilliant, borrowing a structure from Shakespeare, because suddenly all the other characters became clearer. But I didn't want the parallels to be rigid, because the connection could be quite intimidating for some people. If you get something extra from it, that's fine, but the play exists in its own right. In fact, some people who read it early on didn't see the connections, and I liked that. The choice was whether to kill Felix or not. I thought when I started to write that he would have to die, but then I just couldn't kill him. I kind of fell in love with him, but also, by the time I got to that point in the play, it seemed wrong. So although the original image is still intact, it now has a slightly different emphasis.

Once I thought of Felix as a Hamlet figure, I wanted him to be a student, or perhaps a research fellow. I wondered what he could be studying at the age of thirty-five, which would not make him a completely tragic figure. Then I heard a radio talk by an expert in super-string theory. What attracted me was the language he used, he was so passionate about it, and so spiritual. So Felix became a theoretical astrophysicist. The attraction wasn't so much the science as this unified field theory, which combined the big things and the small things. I thought it a perfect match for Felix's life, for his search for unity.

I had to do a lot of research for the science. I'd done one term of physics at school and I didn't even know what an atom was when I started to read around the subject. But I'm quite good at cramming information and assimilating it quickly – and then forgetting it six months later. Actually, there isn't that much science in the play, it's not like Tom Stoppard or anything.

I wrote the character of Felix for Simon Russell Beale, though I never thought he would play it. I had this man who was bumbling around and had an amazing brain, and I thought he was the only actor who could play it. I didn't know him at all, but while I was writing the play I saw him at the National in *Battle Royal* and *Summerfolk*, and that was very inspiring.

Although the play is a comedy, I'm rather wary of calling it that. I think sometimes comedies aren't taken as seriously as other kinds of play and it seems like a hostage to fortune. I suppose it's a tragi-comedy if you want to attach a label. But comedy is what I write, I can't avoid making jokes. I don't have such a bleak world view as Sarah Kane: my instinct is always to find the funny side of things.

Humble Boy opened in the Cottesloe in August 2001.

Challenging scenarios

Martin Crimp discusses his widely performed and controversial *Attempts on her Life*

'All writers have inside themselves a particular seam, which they're going to end up mining, regardless of what it is.

It's just something we have to pursue.'

Martin Crimp's seam is a harsh but fruitful one. His distinctive, challenging plays tend to deal with tough, often cruel subjects – abduction, child abuse, violence, war, pornography. He loves to experiment with form, to explore many different dramatic possibilities. *Attempts on her Life* is a characteristic work: written ten years ago and subsequently put on in numerous European countries, it's considered by many to be the finest of his ten stage plays.

Subtitled '17 Scenarios for the Theatre', on the surface it's about film people brainstorming ideas and telling stories connected with a character called Anna, whom we never see. But its author insists this is merely a device. 'It enabled me to find a technique for writing, a ladder I could then discard,' he says. 'The play is definitely not about the way the media perceives and processes the world, but about the way we as individuals in our privileged Western European culture do so.'

Formally his play offers a unique challenge: the script gives no indication as to who speaks the dialogue, or the number of actors required to perform it – although he does ask that the composition of the company should reflect the composition of the world outside the theatre. 'I didn't want to limit a director, I wanted it to be very open,' he explains. 'Partly I suppose I was resisting the kind of control of the images on stage exercised by Beckett, and later his estate, which to me is very anti-theatre.'

An accomplished musician as well as a playwright, Crimp lays great stress on getting the rhythm of his dialogue right. 'When I write I always speak the words aloud, I try out every line. So the musicality is always important. But in a play like this, made up of seventeen movements if you like, so too is a sense of symmetry and balance. That's why I resist it if a director asks if he or she can change the order of the scenarios.'

The play has been given productions all over Europe, including one at the Piccolo Theatre in Milan in 1999 directed by Katie Mitchell, who is in charge of the National's new production. Yet despite his popularity abroad, Martin Crimp resists the notion that he is essentially a European writer. 'I don't like the word European, because I think all artists gather their strength from their local culture,' he says. 'I see myself as an English writer who was born in Kent, spent his adolescence in Yorkshire and then moved to London. The idea of a European play is rather a scary one, as if it was written to please all tastes and not grounded in reality.'

Although he believes *Attempts on her Life* has an existence separate from the time in which it was written, he acknowledges that it also has a relationship with today. 'It's not a play that needs to chase the present, or be changed for the time that it's being staged in. But its shape and structure do seem to anticipate the concept of globalisation, which was not so current in 1997. And having a scenario called THE THREAT OF INTERNATIONAL TERRORISM® is clearly going to chime with the present.'

Attempts on her Life opened in the Lyttelton in March 2007.

Children in mind

Alan Ayckbourn on *Mr A´s Amazing Maze Plays* and writing for a younger audience

Why should Britain's most successful and prolific living playwright turn his hand to writing for children? By way of answer, Alan Ayckbourn recalls the time when his two young sons used to come and see his adult plays.

'They sat quite happily watching them and a little germ began to form in my mind. I began to see that you don't have to throw your brain out of the window when you write for children. You just use a different set of muscles. More and more parents began to bring children to my adult plays and often they enjoyed them more than the adults did. So I realised you could still write about issues for a younger audience.'

Mr A's Amazing Maze Plays, first performed in Scarborough in 1988 and coming to the National in March, was not his first play for children. In the 1960s he wrote two, but they were unsuccessful and turned him off the genre for a while. Since

Mr A's, however, he has written three more and is planning another for next year. 'What I aim to do is write something that I would like to have seen when I was a child myself. The basic ingredients are the same as for adults: character, storyline and making sure the "And then . . .?" factor is there. But you've just got to do it better, otherwise the kids turn round and start talking. The biggest enemy for them is boredom.'

The narrative device in *Mr A's* aims quite literally to keep the audience involved. The play tells how a young girl Suzy and her dog Neville thwart the attempts of the sinister Mr Accousticus to steal people's voices and keep them in his Cabinet of Sounds. As Suzy and Neville conduct a search of Mr A's empty house, the two narrators repeatedly ask the audience to vote on which room the characters should enter next. Aside from its dramatic purpose, it's a device that reflects Ayckbourn's interest in allowing his characters or the audience to make the choices. 'I want people to realise that live theatre can offer a choice,' he says. 'I try and leave the door open in my children's plays: I have this naïve hope children might have a solution to things locked inside them. So I try to say that anything is possible – within reason of course.'

There is often a thematic link between his adult plays and those he writes for children – for example, *Woman in Mind* and his only other children's play to be staged at the National, *Invisible Friends*. He says that *Mr A's* can be seen 'as a kind of mad version of *Sisterly Feelings*' – in that play there are four possible versions of the action, determined by one random and one deliberate choice. In fact *Mr A's* was written at the same time as his dark, brutal and high-tech play *Henceforward*, and both reflect his preoccupation with technology. 'At the time I was interested in how you can play around with sound,' he says. 'So I decided I wanted to write about some kind of mad sound engineer. That was the starting point for *Mr A's*.'

He believes the play is exciting because even the actors don't know what is going to happen in the scenes in Mr A's house. One especially nervous moment is when Suzy and Neville have to retrace their exact steps to get out of the house. 'At

Scarborough the actors held their breath, because they never remembered the order in which they went in. But the children did, every single time, without fail.'

Some years ago Ayckbourn said he felt he owed it to his characters to let them dictate to a certain extent how a play should run. Did this hold good for writing children's plays? '*Mr A's* was my first real walk along the plank, so I laid it out very carefully,' he explains. 'It did develop as it went along; but my most recent children's plays have been more liberating.'

Despite its narrative originality, *Mr A's* is a wry, rather genteel, very English play: with the dog and a father who flies in and out of the action, there's more than a hint of *Peter Pan*. Ayckbourn says that any such influence is quite unconscious: 'But with this kind of writing all kinds of emotional hardware comes out of the drawer. People look at you and say, "Oh, what kind of childhood did *you* have then?"'

He's very aware that he and other playwrights are having to compete for children's attention with the excitement and special effects available on television and video. He believes, though, that writers too often underestimate children's intelligence. 'We always assume they want to laugh their heads off,' he says. 'But often they're at their happiest when they're sitting seriously, or even in tears.'

In Scarborough, where he runs the Stephen Joseph Theatre and premieres all his plays, he uses the term 'family theatre' rather than 'children's theatre'. 'I'm not interested in having serried ranks of children, and adults using the theatre as a crèche while they go somewhere else. I want them all to come.' He recalls the time when two pensioners booked into one of his children's shows by mistake: 'They had the time of their lives joining in and sharing the children's bullseyes. That's how it should be.'

Mr A's Amazing Maze Plays opened in the Cottesloe in March 1993.

Victims of history

David Hare reflects on his trilogy about the
Church, the criminal justice system and politics

'Of all the groups that I met, I think the judges were the most
socially irresponsible. I found it hard to have any sympathy
with them.'

The judiciary would seem to be the odd group out on David
Hare's research list. For three years he has been taking a hard
look at the commanding institutions of British life. In *Racing
Demon*, *Murmuring Judges* and now *The Absence of War*, he has
managed to get inside the lives of an impressive array of people
working within these institutions and to look sympathetically
at their situation, even while implicitly criticising their
behaviour or values.

One explanation for this even-handedness can be put down
to the process he went through before starting to write. For
each of the three plays, soon to be staged as a trilogy at the
National, he carried out extensive research, gaining access to
places not normally granted to outsiders. For *Racing Demon* he
attended the Synod and talked to clergymen as well as laity.
For *Murmuring Judges* he was a fly on the wall at a police
station, while for *The Absence of War* – which centres on a
general election – he was allowed to sit in on the Labour
Party's election strategy meetings last spring.

The experience changed his perception of many of the
groups he met. 'I'd lost touch with the Church, so I was
surprised to find the degree to which vicars had become social
workers,' he recalls. 'If you imagine that spreading the gospel
to individual souls is what Christian vicars practise, it's very
shocking to find them going out of their way not to mention
Jesus – but also to find that they're doing society's dirty work,
the work that social workers and teachers and politicians are
failing to do.'

What about the police: hadn't they minded having a writer
sitting in the corner, taking down evidence, possibly against
them? 'The police are used to being observed, they know just

how to deal with playwrights,' he says. 'More than any other group – except perhaps politicians – they're skilled at presenting one side to you and another to each other. It's what they strikingly call "an overcoat of values".' The Met were apparently keen that he shouldn't go to Brixton or Notting Hill, which they saw as special cases. He accepted this, since that wasn't what he was looking for. 'I felt that the process of the law was in shades of grey rather than black and white. I wanted to go to a place where most of the crime wasn't trivial, but where there weren't any special problems.' He ended up in Clapham.

The most surprising thing he found in his researches was the politicisation of the police. 'Far from being grateful for the money Thatcher had thrown at them, they were very bitter, because they felt she had created social problems, which they were being left to clear up,' he says. 'Something very strange must be happening when you get the police cold-shouldering a Tory Home Secretary and giving Roy Hattersley a standing ovation.'

And the politicians? 'They were more trapped than I expected. The room for manoeuvre they had, or felt they had, was alarmingly small. They were completely victims of history, or of what they felt history to be. It was quite frightening.' Initially he'd wanted to cover both sides of the election in researching *The Absence of War*. But as soon as he attended his first Labour strategy meeting, he realised there'd be no possibility of any link-up between the two sides. So he concentrated on the opposition party, making his protagonist a leader 'whose qualities come from his passion'.

In all three plays, but especially in *The Absence of War*, the question of a profession's image is raised. But Hare has no truck with the view that it was public relations that decided the 1992 election. 'The idea that it was about glitz and packaging is incredibly shallow and naïve. But it's what that packaging is expressing, rather than the packaging itself, that I wanted to look at.' He agrees that, in writing this type of documentary play, there is sometimes a tension between the pressure to inform and the need and desire to create full-blooded characters. 'In *Murmuring Judges* the structuring of the play into three parts was so complicated, I did have to simplify and take short cuts, so some of the characters aren't as well developed as others.'

He doesn't think of the three works as 'condition of England' plays, but as an attempt to deal with questions of the 1980s arising from Mrs Thatcher's efforts to denigrate or abolish institutions, notably trade unions. 'We need institutions, and we need them to be run in the interests of the people who work in them and use them,' he says. 'I don't know how you express the common good except through institutions. I want to see them refreshed; a well-run institution is a beautiful thing. But at present they're not well run and we're having a national nervous breakdown about whether they can be.'

And those judges? 'Murmuring judges' means to speak ill of the judiciary, still an offence in Scotland. Safely south of the border, Hare recalls a meeting with one judge: 'He actually said to me, "I can't go into a prison, because I'd then be able to imagine where I was sending these people." That to me is an almost criminally irresponsible attitude.'

The Absence of War opened in the Olivier in September 1993.

Comedy of desire

Hanif Kureishi returns to the theatre with his sharp satire *Sleep With Me*

When the idea for *Sleep With Me* first came to Hanif Kureishi, he thought he was going mad. 'A few years ago, on holiday in Italy, I woke up in the middle of the night,' he recalls. 'I had an image of people on stage, arriving in a garden, people talking and rushing about, darkness falling. It made me very nervous, it wouldn't go away, it stayed in my mind. So eventually I wrote a play about it.'

Set during a summer weekend in a house in the countryside, the result is a fast-moving, tragi-comic satire exposing the emotionally and sexually chaotic lives of people working in the media. Any resemblance to Ingmar Bergman's film *Smiles of a Summer Night* and Woody Allen's homage to it, *A Midsummer Night's Sex Comedy*, is not entirely coincidental. 'Yes, I was influenced by those two films,' Kureishi admits. 'The idea of the magic of the night, of coming together with people you don't know very well, having conversations you wouldn't normally have, how lives can be changed overnight. I think that's where the idea came from.'

Sleep With Me, Kureishi's first play for the National, marks a return to theatre after a fifteen-year break. What with *My Beautiful Launderette*, *The Buddha of Suburbia*, other film and television work, plus novels and short stories, it's easy to forget that he had considerable success as a young playwright, with work being staged at the Royal Court, Hampstead, Riverside Studios and the Soho Poly. 'I stopped writing for the theatre partly because I felt I didn't have anything to contribute in the way of form,' he says. 'But writing this play, with its broken-up, cinematic style, was an interesting challenge – though it was exhausting to write, and took a lot of emotional juice and energy.'

He claims that attacking media people is not his main purpose. 'They're no more foolish than people who drive buses,' he says. 'I wanted to write a play about marriage, about the difficulty of sustaining relationships in the long term, about the cost of doing so and what happens when they go wrong.' Much of *Sleep With Me* is about sex, a subject he sees as full of possibilities for humour. 'Ideally we should desire the people we are supposed to desire, but unfortunately desire mocks us and makes us behave in ways that rationally we would not want to. Desire can be very comic.'

He hesitated over the explicitly sexual title, wondering whether to call the play simply *Weekend*. 'But it's not just about a sexual proposition. And sleeping with someone isn't necessarily having sex with them, it's often more intimate than that. So I rather liked the ambiguity.' One foil to the media characters is Barry, the politicised schoolteacher. 'I suppose he's an old leftie and after 1989 that can seem ridiculous,' Kureishi reflects. 'So on the one hand he is rather absurd; but on the other hand he seems to believe in stuff that has gripped the imagination for most of our century. It's easy to be dismissive of such people.'

After the isolation of novel writing he's keen to do another play, though he's got no particular subject in mind. 'What I do is put my aerial up and after a time I get an idea.' He admits to being wary of commissions, having some outstanding from the 1980s. 'If someone asks me to do something, I'm the sort of person who's quite likely to do the opposite.'

Sleep With Me opened in the Cottesloe in April 1999.

Starting from scratch

Matthew Bourne on the creation of *Play Without Words*

The Transformation season at the National last year was the ideal chance to do something experimental like *Play Without Words*. It was the right atmosphere, it felt right being part of a bigger idea. It was very scary, having no script and just a few pieces of music. But any commission like that, where you are free to do what you want, you grab at it, because such chances are rare.

My composer Terry Davies and I wanted to see how far you could go in telling a story without using words. The inspiration was the British new-wave film and theatre of the early 1960s, in particular Joseph Losey's *The Servant*. We thought the score could be jazz influenced, because so many films of the time seemed to use this music to create atmosphere. It was all very vague at the start: there was little plot, we just jotted down a number of themes that linked with the characters and their feelings.

I remember thinking on day one of rehearsals, 'Oh my God, all we're doing is walking round the room improvising and in five weeks we've got the public coming in.' Gradually we added bits, but we had no idea what we were going to come up with. Fortunately you're very protected at the National, you're surrounded by many more people than usual, helping you to achieve what you want to. So if you suddenly decide you need a new prop, it's often there ten minutes later.

We had decided that each of the main characters would be played by three different actor/dancers at the same time, which was perhaps a difficult concept. When acted out in the Studio without costumes or lighting, the story seemed really confusing. Fortunately Mick Gordon, the director of the season, and our producer Joe Smith stayed with it, and we got there just in time. The first preview was very scary: I was still creating the last scene while the audience were waiting to come in.

But the response was incredible and I was very happy with it. We had a good cross-section in the audience: it wasn't just a dance audience, it also seemed to appeal to the established National audience, who I find are pretty open-minded to any new kind of work. It wasn't sold hard up front, it caught on by word of mouth, so in the last two weeks of its four-week run it was totally full, which was exciting.

I can't imagine anywhere else but the National that would have agreed to stage our piece with the very limited ideas we initially gave them. Now that it's coming back to the Lyttelton there are inevitably a few changes I want to make. Since we have a little more time, we need to look again at certain sections of the piece – some of which were completed in a single afternoon.

Play Without Words opened in the Lyttelton in December 2003.

The loveliest job in the world

Jim Cartwright on his highly original
The Rise and Fall of Little Voice

The creator of *Road*, *Bed* and *To* describes his latest play as being about ordinary folk doing extraordinary things. 'I like to write about the magic in ordinary life,' he says.

Little Voice is certainly no ordinary character. A young girl trapped at home with a selfish, drunken mother, she lives a lonely fantasy life, listening to and imitating records of songs sung by Piaf, Garland, Dietrich and other artists. Silent for most of the play, she has revenge on her mother in an extraordinary denouement. Jim Cartwright got the idea from knowing actress Jane Horrocks, who plays Little Voice, and who in real life can do impersonations. 'I was also thinking about terrifying things, like waking up and finding your voice wasn't there. So I began to write and the story started to unfold.'

Like his earlier work, *The Rise and Fall of Little Voice* is a potent mixture of humour, raw emotion and underlying tragedy, written in a language that is at once crude and strangely poetic. Yet although it reflects conflict within a working-class family, it is not an overtly political play. 'I'm more of a humanist writer, although sometimes the politics just creeps in,' Cartwright says. He also sees the play as a journey of discovery, in which a person suffering finds her voice.

It seems an apt metaphor. He himself did so theatrically six years ago when the Royal Court unexpectedly commissioned him to write *Road*, a hard-hitting piece that won him many awards. 'It was a real shock, but also very encouraging,' he says. Although he had created 'little poems for myself' ever since he could remember, he had only written scenes rather than a full-length play when a friend persuaded him to send some of them to the Court. 'I had an inner feeling that they were good, but I never thought that others would think that,' he remembers. 'I thought writing was what clever people did.'

His Lancashire home was no literary household, though his mother – who died recently – read quite a lot. His father worked in a factory and now, aged eighty, comes to all his son's plays. He himself left school at sixteen. 'I'm not well read or anything like that,' he says.

So do his plays reach beyond the traditional middle-class audiences? He's not sure if *Bed* did so at the National, but there was certainly a more mixed crowd when *Road* was performed at the Bolton Octagon. 'It got a bit cultish, people came to see it four times,' he recalls with pleasure. 'We had punk rockers in with shaven heads, and people would come up to me after the show and ask me to sign their UB40s.'

A lot of the words in *Little Voice* are ones he made up himself. 'They just come out and sometimes I'm not sure if they're words at all. But if they fit the meaning, I leave it.' Like other instinctive writers, he has his bad days. 'When nothing comes, it's terrible,' he says. 'On other days, writing plays is the loveliest job in the world.'

The Rise and Fall of Little Voice opened in the Cottesloe in June 1992.

Your own history

Winsome Pinnock on *Leave Taking*, language and black culture

'I feel that very strongly, that sense of being between two cultures, of not being quite sure where your home is, where you really belong.' Such uncertainties are familiar to playwright Winsome Pinnock. Although she was born and brought up in England, her parents were originally from Jamaica. It's a background of which she makes subtle and powerful use in *Leave Taking*.

The play centres on the relationship between a mother and her two daughters. It embraces the kind of inter-generational conflicts, emotional battles and comic misunderstandings that can be found in most families. But it's also rooted in a very specific black English culture, where memories of or dreams about the Caribbean exert a strong influence on the family. This is reflected in the play's language, which consists partly of Jamaican dialect, but of a kind that's comprehensible to white audiences. 'I would question all that stuff about authenticity,' Winsome Pinnock says. 'Every writer uses language in their own way. I like writing in dialect, because it changes all the time. I don't use it myself, but it's somewhere there inside me. It's also to do with acknowledging your own history.'

She's been writing for ten years, and has had residencies at the Royal Court and the Tricycle. *Leave Taking* is in fact her first play, written at the prompting of Hanif Kureishi. 'I didn't know a thing about writing plays and I asked him what you had to do,' she recalls. 'He gave me a deadline and told me to write eight scenes of fifteen minutes each. So I did.' She subsequently revised the play for the Liverpool Playhouse, where it was first performed in 1987. She remembers getting positive comments from young women in the audience: 'That's exactly my story,' one said. They came from white as well as black women. 'The important thing about plays is that they lead people into another world, they make connections between them,' Pinnock says.

Paulette Randall, who's directing *Leave Taking*, believes it will get a good response from young audiences of all backgrounds and cultures. 'Whoever you are, between sixteen and twenty-five you're trying to assert yourself, you're against someone in authority, so it will hit everyone,' she suggests. Both women believe it's a positive step for black playwrights that such a work is being staged by the National. 'It's important that plays by black writers get into the mainstream,' Pinnock says. 'Too often it seems to come down to marketing, to a feeling that such plays won't fill the space.'

Randall argues that black writers have been ghettoised for too long. 'They none of them want to be like this, that's not what they write for,' she says. 'But for years their plays have mainly been put on in small theatres or local halls, so most people just don't get a chance to see them.' Now, come the New Year, audiences all around England – and parts of Northern Ireland – will have a chance to catch up with a fresh, humane and finely wrought play, that has clearly found its way into the National's repertoire on merit.

Leave Taking opened in the Cottesloe in January 1995 and then toured.

Mining a rich seam

Sebastian Barry lifts 'the great cloth of silence' from his family's history in *Our Lady of Sligo*

Sebastian Barry never met his grandmother. He's tried several times in recent years to tackle her story. Only now, with the intensely moving *Our Lady of Sligo*, has he succeeded. 'Entering her world was hard because it involved childhood fears,' he says. 'All I had was a demonic remnant of her life told to me by my mother. I tried without success to use it in my first play. Then I attempted to put it into a short novel. But as soon as I touched it, my life went into reverse. I was afraid she was malign.'

His previous play, the magnificent award-winning *The Steward of Christendom*, covered the life of his great-grandfather. *Our Lady of Sligo* also centres on a family situation, with the characters – which include both his grandmother and mother – delving into their turbulent past and attempting to come to terms with it. Both plays are part of a series in which Barry has consciously gone in search of the lost, hidden or seldom-mentioned members of his Irish family. 'I felt a great cloth of silence had been thrown over them, for political or social reasons,' he says. 'You have to acknowledge all your ancestors.'

As in the earlier work, the action of *Our Lady of Sligo* is punctuated by lengthy monologues, full of wistful and anguished poetic imagery. Intriguingly, Barry argues that 'the monologues are really dialogues, with the other person not answering', but admits that 'my plays are peculiar objects, which don't seem to fit into what you might call Proper Theatre'. He says he doesn't believe in writing as such. 'It's more a question of listening and waiting for the material to make sense. It often turns up in alarming fashion as characters take their own course; but you have to follow their line without prejudice.'

Now forty-two, he's been writing for twenty years, though initially he concentrated on fiction and poetry. Theatre he saw as the territory of his mother Joan O'Hara, an actress at the

Abbey in Dublin. So he steered clear of writing plays until 1986, when his first one was performed – at the Abbey. He claims to have written the first draft while his actress wife was away for two weeks working in *Casualty*. 'I'd read that Lorca could write a play in a fortnight, so I thought, why not?' After that, other commissions came rolling in – from the Abbey, then the Bush and finally from Max Stafford-Clark at the Royal Court.

Last year he was a Writer Fellow at Trinity College in Dublin, where he was once a student. Teaching seems not to be his vocation. 'After twenty years living on halfpennies and pound notes, I saw everyone else as the competition. So my instinct was to put poison in the students' coffee. I also thought, "What can I teach them? Who wants to write like me? Isn't one enough?"'

Pressed about the nature of his next play, he admits that the rich seam of family history he has been mining may finally be exhausted. 'Something has come full circle with *Sligo* and I think perhaps I should be moving on to other concerns.'

Our Lady of Sligo opened in the Cottesloe in April 1998.

A theatrical bonanza

David Eldridge fills in the personal background to *Market Boy*

Last year was quite a year for David Eldridge. His acclaimed adaptation of the controversial Dogme95 film *Festen* was followed by a stunning modern version of Ibsen's *The Wild Duck*, both shows enjoying sell-out runs respectively at the Almeida and the Donmar. Now an ambitious play of his own is about to explode on to the main stage at the National.

Market Boy is based on Eldridge's experiences in the 1980s in Romford Market, where he worked on a stall selling women's shoes. It was, he remembers, 'an unworldly thirteen-year-old's rites-of-passage journey to adulthood'. On the way he mastered the art of selling stilettos, meanwhile 'learning a good wind-up, discovering sex, alcohol and drugs and the temptations of money, all in the company of a brigand band of wild teenagers and my boss, the market's answer to Don Juan'.

The resulting play is an exhilarating epic story of a teenager's initiation into the harsh and savage world of Essex traders. It's a work full of crime, laughter, sadness, guilt, heartbreak and much else. 'It's a smorgasbord of a show,' Eldridge says, 'a mixture of dirty realism, Jonsonian comedy and circus, inspired by the Britflick, *The Mysteries*, *The Jungle Book*, the Broadway musical and plays at the Royal Court. It's also about the time when Mrs Thatcher said we should all embrace the market place.'

Now well established as a playwright, his original ambition when he was at university – he studied English and Drama at Exeter – was to be a director. 'But I didn't pursue that because there were certain things I wanted to express, which I could only do by writing my own plays.' Before his two recent successes, his work was staged at the Bush, Hampstead and the Royal Court. But to have a play on this subject performed on a stage as large as the Olivier is the fulfilment of a long-held dream.

'I'd often thought about dramatising those market experiences, but a realistic work-play with a permanent set seemed inappropriate and I didn't want it to turn into some kind of glorified *EastEnders*. I also felt that the scale on which I wanted to write the play made the idea impossible to achieve in a smaller theatre. It's a problem that faces many of the playwrights of my generation, who have trouble in moving on from the black-box studios.'

Market Boy is a vibrant, helter-skelter of a play, containing some forty characters. It began its life four years ago in the unlikely setting of a bar in Johannesburg. Here Eldridge found himself telling stories about his Romford days to the National's literary manager Jack Bradley and Mick Gordon, director of the Transformation season at the National. Although there was some talk of it being included in that ground-breaking season of new work, it was finally decided to give it a sustained period of development, with Rufus Norris, who was also responsible for *Festen*, coming in as director.

'A market is a very theatrical world, so I could see it was full of potential for the stage,' Norris says. 'It's now become a very strong, very human story, and a good deal of fun: the audience will get a very unpolitically correct, ribald, gaudy show. But it's also a play with a more serious side, which looks at questions such as the loss of innocence and how life really was in the market-driven eighties, the climate in which David and I grew up.'

Over the last three years director and writer have worked on the play with different groups of actors in the National's Studio. After Eldridge wrote down his stories and the actors read them aloud, they were then set aside, and the actors gradually built up a fictional narrative and a substantial collection of characters. 'Autobiography can be a useful starting point, but it doesn't make a play,' Eldridge observes. 'Sometimes it just becomes an awful kind of therapy, and not good art.'

The process involved a lot of improvisation, with the actors being 'hot-seated', and creating characters from ideas fed to them by Eldridge and Norris. At one point they set up an actual market in the Studio, with proper stalls and real fruit and shoes, and improvised possible scenes. 'As we tested the material, a lot of imaginations were fired and the play began to take on a life of its own,' Eldridge recalls. 'After writing on my own, it was a joy to work in this collaborative way. It makes you less precious about your words – although I'm sure I'll play the writer card in a more steely way when we come to rehearsals.'

Popular music is an important element of the show, as Eldridge has woven many evocative 1980s songs into the action. 'I always listen to songs when I'm working, and often they end up in the play – though they also often get cut.' The line-up for *Market Boy* may change, but at present it includes the music of groups such as Frankie Goes to Hollywood, The Stone Roses, Funboy Three, Bananarama, Everything But the Girl and Dexy's Midnight Runners.

Both writer and director are excited at the thought of staging the play in the Olivier. 'It feels like getting an England cap or playing in a cup final, but you just have to concentrate on the work,' Eldridge says. 'I love the open space, the way it draws you in. It's also ideal for driving vans on and off.' Norris, for whom this is also a National debut, is buoyant about working in such a theatre: 'It's a tricky space and directors more experienced than me have occasionally failed in it. But I think it's ideal for a theatrical bonanza such as *Market Boy*. I can't wait to get started.'

Market Boy opened in the Olivier Theatre in May 2006.

The eternal triangle

Nick Stafford discusses *Battle Royal*, his investigation of a disastrous royal marriage

The story seems vaguely familiar: a prince who is heir to the throne, his unhappy wife and Another Woman. But Nick Stafford denies his latest work has anything directly to do with the disintegrating relationships of the present-day royal family. 'Any modern echoes that you hear were largely unconscious,' he says. 'I was focusing on George and Caroline, whose story is fascinating in itself. Anyway, I can't imagine anyone will look at Simon Russell Beale and Zoë Wanamaker and think, there go Charles and Diana.'

The eternal triangle in *Battle Royal*, which is being directed by Howard Davies, features the Prince of Wales (who soon becomes George IV), his wife Caroline of Brunswick, and the other woman, Mrs Fitzherbert. Clearly the play will have a certain extra buzz around it because of recent events within the Windsor family and because of people's continuing fascination with royalty. But the earlier Hanoverian story is one that has long interested Stafford. 'I read about it when I was young, in Churchill's *A History of the English-Speaking Peoples*, so when today's royal marriages started to fall apart I thought, this has happened before. I think if we knew our history better, we wouldn't be so taken by surprise. Everything that happens started some time ago.'

Stafford doesn't subscribe to the normal view of libertine George as a total monster. 'I have to forgive him and love him, otherwise I wouldn't be able to write him,' he says. 'In any case I think to a certain extent he was trapped. One of the themes of the play is how you live when you're surrounded by so many rules, and what you do when there's only certain people you can marry.' Although he makes Caroline of Brunswick a strong, feisty character, he was not consciously writing a feminist play. 'I wasn't making a special case for anybody; I was just trying to think what their situations were and give them equal weight. Of course, Caroline had disadvantages because she was a woman. She could have gone under several times, but she was very tough.'

Although he's delved into biographies of her, he's still had to imagine what she was like in private. 'I haven't invented anything that couldn't have happened, but I have used some poetic licence with the facts,' he admits. While sticking closely to the known story, for the sake of dramatic tightness he's telescoped the timescale and merged the actions of certain characters.

Despite the spotlight on George and Caroline, *Battle Royal* is as much about government as about the monarchy. It shows how the personalities of those in power affected the decisions they made during this time of near civil war. The tumultuous events it records – including the queen being tried for adultery – have allowed Stafford the rare luxury of a broad canvas. 'It's been a fantastic freedom not to have to worry about the number of characters,' he confesses. 'For instance, one key scene – showing the House of Lords, gangs of men in the street and lawyers in court – has twenty-five people on stage at the same time. If the play had been a two-hander they'd be talking about the things that had happened, but I can actually show them happening.'

Comparisons will inevitably be made with Alan Bennett's *The Madness of George III*, a huge success at the National at the beginning of the decade. Nick Stafford would prefer them not to be: 'When someone said *Battle Royal* could be a sequel to it, I was really shocked. It's not that at all, it's completely different, dramatically and in every other way.' He's delighted with the casting of the two leading parts. 'Simon played George when the play was read at the Studio. He's got something of the class, he's the right shape and he's very, very funny. And Zoë Wanamaker is absolutely right for Caroline: she won't play her as a victim, and it's very important that she avoids self-pity.'

Battle Royal opened in the Lyttelton in December 1999.

Getting there

Patrick Marber and Paul Godfrey reveal how they made it to the National

Although the authors of the two new plays in the Cottesloe got there by very different routes and from very different backgrounds, they both did so via directing, and both feel that luck played a big part in their achievement. 'I was just in the right place at the right time,' says Patrick Marber, author of *Dealer's Choice*, his first play for the stage. Paul Godfrey, whose *The Blue Ball* is his second play at the National, admits, 'I feel as if I've had a terrific struggle, but I realise that I've actually been very lucky.'

Their previous experience could hardly be more of a contrast. Marber has been a stand-up comic and has written comedy scripts for television, including *The Day Today* and *Knowing Me, Knowing You*. 'I'd always wanted to write for the stage, but never quite got round to it,' he says. Godfrey, on the other hand, came to writing after five years of directing plays in Scotland. After a spell as a trainee at Perth Theatre, he directed new plays for a company based in Inverness, which toured them round the Highlands and Islands. 'Working alongside those writers made me realise I too wanted to write,' he says.

He began in traditional fashion, collecting rejection slips from more than thirty theatres for his first play. But then both the Royal Court and the National accepted unsolicited work from him. 'It had seemed arrogant to send them there, but I realised that I should have been braver,' he confesses. *The Blue Ball*, an original and distinctive play about the lives of astronauts and their experience of space, was actually commissioned by the National. But he had to raise grant money elsewhere to finance what he saw as essential research trips to the USA and the former Soviet Union, where he met several astronauts and, at Cape Canaveral, witnessed live the launch of a space shuttle.

Directing in Patrick Marber's case involved a comedy show, which won a Perrier award at the Edinburgh Fringe. This brought him to the attention of staff at the National's Studio, who gave him the use of six actors for two weeks, and the opportunity to develop with them his idea for a play centring on a game of poker. The result was a Studio production of a first draft of *Dealer's Choice*, followed by an offer to take a final version into the Cottesloe.

He talks approvingly of the freedom he's been given by the National, being allowed both to direct and cast his play, and choose the designer. 'I think it helped that I had a small cast and a low budget,' he says. 'Creating the play was a collaborative process. I was lucky to work with such a talented group of actors, some of whom are in the final cast. Really we mapped out the scenes together.' The result, after four drafts, is a comic but poignant piece – its author calls it a 'domestic tragedy' – that uses poker to explore issues such as power, sexism, male friendships, and the relationship between fathers and sons.

So what else is needed, apart from luck and ability? Godfrey is clear about the answer. 'What's most difficult when you're starting out is to have the faith that someone will be interested, or that what you're saying is at all significant.' In a climate where new writers often have to struggle for years before getting a play performed anywhere, his and Marber's stories offer encouragement to others trying to make their mark. They also provide an antidote to the widely held belief that it's hard to get a play on unless you have the right contacts, know an established director, or are already involved with a theatre.

Dealer's Choice opened in the Cottesloe in February 1995, *The Blue Ball* in March 1995.

Part Two

Adaptations and Musicals

Time present and time past

Harold Pinter talks about adapting Marcel Proust's famous novel for the theatre

Sitting in the small, square house in Holland Park that he uses as an office, Harold Pinter recalls a moment of truth from nearly thirty years ago. Having agreed to write the screenplay for Joseph Losey's film version of Proust's *A la recherche du temps perdu* and made copious notes on the epic seven-volume novel, it was time to get something down on paper.

'I went to my study and sat there. The next morning I was still sitting there. I called Joe Losey and said, "I simply can't start." He said, "Walk round the block." So I walked round the block and came back. The next morning it was exactly the same: I was still sitting there looking at a blank piece of paper. So I called him again and said, "This is terrible, I simply can't start." And he said, "There's only one thing to do" and I said, "What's that?" And he said, "*Start!*" So like a puppet I immediately wrote something down. I began to explore those extraordinary images in Proust of sound and vision, which come back to haunt him.'

Pinter has described the time he spent on the screenplay in 1972 as the best working year of his life. Talking during rehearsals for the stage version at the National, *Remembrance of Things Past*, he still looks back at it with obvious pleasure. 'I had read the first volume, *Swann's Way*, earlier in my life and had always meant to return to the novel. So I sat down and read Proust for three solid months, without doing anything else, reading it every day. It was quite wonderful really, I was quite overwhelmed by it.'

As with the stage adaptation, his aim was to catch the essence of Proust's vast work rather than come up with a condensed version of the novel. 'The book had already been written, you couldn't write it again,' he says. 'What we were concerned about was how to give it an accurate, true and faithful distillation.' So how did he find a structural way through the 3,300-page novel? 'We knew early on that a number of characters would have to go. We also thought there were two main parts, one going if you like towards disillusion, age and death, the other towards revelation, imagination and art.'

Sadly, the film was never made. Although the main problem was raising the money, there were also difficulties over casting. While Pinter wanted to use only English actors, potential backers from several European countries wanted their own actors to appear in the film. 'You could have ended up with a terrible pudding of actors speaking three thousand different dialects, in broken English,' he suggests. 'I didn't like the sound of that at all.'

His work was not wasted, however, being published as *The Proust Screenplay*. The idea of shifting it into another medium came from Di Trevis, director of the National's production and an ardent Proust lover. After a trial run with students at the London Academy of Music and Dramatic Art, her stage version was performed in a rehearsal room at the National, where both Trevor Nunn and Pinter became excited by it. She and Pinter then worked jointly on shaping the current version.

The spell worked on Pinter all over again. 'I went back to Proust, started to sniff around in him, and once I started I couldn't put the book down, I found it extraordinarily hypnotic.' He suggested one significant change to Di Trevis' version. 'She employed a narrator, as in the book, which I thought was a mistake. In my screenplay the narrator had only one sentence, which comes at the very end: "It was time to begin." He then writes the book, as it were. She agreed to the change.'

A surprise in both versions was his decision to omit the celebrated moment when the taste of a *madeleine* dipped in tea brings back to Marcel the memory of his childhood. 'I'm not saying the *madeleine* is a cliché, but I couldn't see how to represent it without it *becoming* a cliché,' he says. 'It doesn't seem to me the most important image in the book, but it's become so from propaganda. People who haven't read the book know about the *madeleine*.'

Proust's preoccupation with time and memory is not unlike

Pinter's and clearly resonates with him. 'One of the most important elements in Proust is how time operates, how time kills really, and how the imagination triumphs by overcoming time. It reminds me very much of John Donne's "Death thou shalt die". It's the triumph of art, if you like. Where Proust suggests that to a certain extent we're locked into ourselves and at the mercy of time, at the moment when the imagination is allowed to live and be fecund, it's defeating time.'

He disagrees roundly with the critics who see Proust as a snob. 'I think that's absolutely ridiculous,' he says. 'In my view he was a merciless satirist, extremely perceptive and acute, and unflinching about the society in which he lived, and showing it in all its most ghastly colours and pretensions. He was quite remorseless in that. He's also very funny – he's really every-thing, an extraordinary man.'

I ask him if his immersion in Proust over the years has had an influence on his own work. His reply is characteristically wary and precise. 'I think it may well have done so, but it's impossible for me to define precisely how. Others might be able to get a better perspective on that. I can't get a distance myself, I can't make any such judgement or measurement. But I'm sure you can't read Proust and not be profoundly affected and influenced by him in one way or another.'

He has 'popped in' to a number of rehearsals at the National. 'I've kept my ear to the ground, listened to the text, made one or two changes. Di is the director, but she consults me when she has to. I have a contribution to make, I think. It's a complex work, but it's being done very simply, indeed very naked – except they'll be wearing clothes. I hope we've done some justice to the texture of the book: that's all one can possibly hope to do.'

Remembrance of Things Past opened in the Cottesloe in November 2000.

Away with naturalism

Helen Edmundson reveals how she adapted
Jamila Gavin's *Coram Boy*

What usually steers me when I start adapting a novel is finding a theme that will engage a modern audience. There's no point in doing the work if it's simply a homage to a book. Normally I spend some time getting to grips with all the ideas the story is dealing with. Then I identify a central driving idea, the idea I want my piece of theatre to explore, and which I want the audience to come out thinking about.

This controls all the decisions I make about where I should focus and where I lose material, and it forms the backbone to the piece. I don't like narrators on stage, I like it to be properly dramatic. As soon as you have a narrator you're admitting that this was once a novel; you're taking a step back from the story.

When working with Shared Experience I have tried to come up with a theatrical device that makes it possible to explore ideas and arguments. In *Anna Karenina*, for example, I had Levin and Anna talk to each other in a kind of no-man's-land space, which I imagined to be the inside of Tolstoy's head. It meant they could debate with each other about their different ways of living, but also tell each other where they were in the story at any given moment, which was useful, especially for such a vast novel.

Coram Boy is very different from the novels I have tackled before. It's a complex narrative, but not a psychologically driven book. It has an almost fairy-tale feel to it and there's something archetypal about a lot of the characters. So I didn't have to find a device that would unlock arguments or debates; I just had to decide how to centre the story so that it would take us on a coherent emotional journey.

I decided to focus on two boys: Alex, the rich boy, and Meshak, who is desperately poor. They have a lot in common: both are very troubled individuals, but through circumstance and the cruelties of the world they end up having completely different life experiences. I wanted to explore the idea that they are almost like alter egos of each other. So, in the first scene of the play they meet – in a glancing sort of way – and from then onwards their two stories wind in and out of each other. They shadow and affect each other without knowing it.

In the novel there isn't that kind of contact between them. Thomas is probably more prominent there – he's funny and attractive, and very much the 'everyman' character. We are introduced to Alexander's wealthy family life through his eyes, which is all very good, and I've kept some of that in. But dramatically Thomas isn't as useful to me, so I've had to slightly reduce him, and find ways of showing how Alex and Meshak are linked. But it didn't need much wrestling to pull that into shape.

I've been quite spoilt working with Shared Experience, because I've always felt that I could write anything and it would be achievable. Happily, Melly Still, the director and co-designer of *Coram Boy*, seems to share my aesthetic. So there's no question of big sets being brought on. She likes an open space, to keep it raw and simple, to be very inventive and to have the actors create things themselves. The scenes are often short and move fluidly in and out of each other, sometimes even overlapping, so there has to be a free and open stage.

In adapting a novel I don't find naturalism particularly useful. The brilliant thing about adaptation is that it forces me to be bold, to put things on stage that I wouldn't necessarily put there if I were writing an original play. Naturalism just has to go out of the window, because it can't cope with the demands of the story.

For example, one challenge with *Coram Boy* was the matter of the dead babies. In the end we decided to use puppets, manipulated quite visibly by the actors. That kind of obviously theatrical convention is incredibly liberating and means I can write anything. If there are things that prove to be impossible then I'll have to rewrite, but doing it this way pushes everyone towards creative solutions.

The music is another essential and exciting ingredient, and I've worked closely with the whole creative team to discover the right musical framework. The key to this was where to put the performance of Handel's *Messiah*, which comes halfway through the second half of the novel. We soon realised that it had to be the climax, that it simply couldn't happen before then. The fact that it's a piece of music that has a child being born, lost and then resurrected is just perfect for our finale.

Making it fluid

Melly Still offers a director's perspective on *Coram Boy*

Once Helen Edmundson had done a draft adaptation of the novel I held some workshops, in order to find a good dramatic form for the piece and an appropriate way to stage it. We were keen to avoid it being plot-driven and expositional, to work on it as a piece of dramatic writing. So Helen had to make some bold decisions.

Because there were two parallel stories, those of Alexander and Meshak, the scenes tumbled into each other, so I needed to find a very fluid way of staging them. Another task was to explore ways of making Meshak's interior world more vivid. We also had to decide about the babies, whether to work with puppets or with sound.

A major question was that of the choirboys: should they be real ones? I felt that women actors, soprano singers playing treble boy singers, would work better. Experienced and talented actresses could hold the stage, whereas it would be more of a risk with children. We still had to do a lot of work training the actresses musically: we brought in a specialist choirmaster, who eventually became the music director.

With a cast of twenty-two, a chamber orchestra and a choir, we never had a problem filling the Olivier stage, as some people thought we might. Once I knew we had the revolve, we used all the space around it. We used every corner of the stage and even burst into the scene dock. Once we started running the play, we realised we had to cut half an hour. So we sat down and ruthlessly cut big sections of it. The actors had to do the cut version the next day, the day before the technical rehearsal. That could have been quite destabilising, but they took it very well and were terribly supportive.

For the revival we've made a few musical and narrative changes, just tightening things up, or making them clearer. Happily, about three-quarters of the original cast are returning. They loved performing the play, partly because it was a new work: it grew with them, so they felt very much part of it.

Coram Boy opened in the Olivier in November 2005, and was revived there in November 2006.

The actress' tale

Prunella Scales is recruiting Chaucer to help counter the neglect of the spoken word

'Chaucer is fascinating: I think the whole feminism theme that goes through *The Canterbury Tales* is quite extraordinary.' Prunella Scales has some individual views about the father of English poetry. Right now she's concentrating on *The Franklin's Tale*. 'I think it's a deeply funny story,' she says. 'Chaucer is very funny about male chauvinism and very good on the snobbery of his men.'

Last year she directed a rehearsed reading of *The Franklin's Tale* in the Cottesloe. The two performances were a sell-out, so the National has asked her to repeat the experiment, this time in the Lyttelton, with a reading of *The Nun's Priest's Tale* to make up a Chaucer double bill. The performances are aimed at students and teachers doing Chaucer, and include a post-show discussion. She recalls that during last year's 'very lively chat' some of the audience felt she had made the story too funny. 'It was perhaps my fault, it was my perception as an actress. But I don't think you demean the story in any way by exploring the hypocrisy.'

On the face of it, it seems surprising that such a busy and successful actress should be willing to give up time for an esoteric venture of this kind. When you talk to her, however, you soon realise how it fits in with her strong views about classical texts and the need for them to be brought alive. But she makes it clear she has no desire to criticise teachers.

'They're the most important people in our whole society, and ludicrously hard-pressed, underpaid and short of time. But I've noticed in some schools that children may be doing exciting improvisatory work in their drama classes, but never touch a classical text, while in their English lessons they may read Chaucer, Milton and Dryden, but never be encouraged to move out from their desks, or read the text aloud to each other. So the whole tradition of the spoken word, the experience of hearing a text and speaking it at the same time – which is the quickest way of learning it – is neglected as a teaching aid, quite apart from the pleasure and stimulus and analytical insight it can give you.'

At a recent session in a school for the National's W. H. Smith Interact scheme, she had the students reading aloud part of *Pride and Prejudice*. 'It was wildly successful, they responded brilliantly,' she recalls. 'The text came alive and you saw an irony in the writing that you simply couldn't see on the page. We're very good at encouraging children to express themselves in their own words, but not so good when it comes to expressing themselves through other people's words.'

She believes the rehearsed readings similarly help to get Chaucer 'off the page'. It's important, she feels, that the actors read from the Middle English text, while using modern pronunciation, so that the text is both familiar to students and accessible to the audience. She is indignant about Chaucer 'translations': 'How can you translate Chaucer, when it's our own language?' But for her the readings are valuable for another reason: they give actors playing small parts and understudying at the National a chance to work on substantial pieces of text. Too often, she argues with some fervour, this aspect of their training is neglected.

'I find increasingly among young actors a lack of fluency in classical texts. It's not their fault, they just don't have the experience of speaking it aloud, and nobody has explained it to them. We have a young generation of staggeringly good actors, and yet the whole tradition of phrasing and delivery is being neglected. I think the drama schools may be falling down a bit there.' She clearly sees her directing work as a small attempt to redress the balance. 'Dare I say it, it's probably quite useful for the actors to work with a jaded old hack like me, who is known, for instance, to be able to get the laughs in a classical text. They're likely to trust my ideas about phrasing – which are extremely rigid.'

This is not her first shot at directing. She has directed intermittently throughout her working life, and at the National had previously staged a rehearsed reading of *She Stoops to Conquer*. She says she finds it 'hugely satisfying', but would never want only to direct. 'One of the satisfactions of being an actor is that you're using your body every night, as well as your brain and emotions. Besides, most directors are twelve, now, and I'm well over twenty-six.' She feels directing has made her a more flexible actress. 'You realise some of the problems and you see things in a more all-round way.' She believes many actors make good directors partly because they have seen so many other directors at work.

If she gets the opportunity, she'd like to give *Paradise Lost* a rehearsed reading, using the famous William Blake drawings as décor. 'I must say I was bored to sobs with Milton at school, but it is wonderful, and I'd like to explore it. I think with the Blakes it could be quite an experience.'

The Chaucer readings took place in the Lyttelton in June 1992.

Going for a song

Jonathan Pryce on the delights of playing Professor Higgins in *My Fair Lady*

'I always seem to be singing these days – but then I do enjoy it so enormously. And I have all these great romantic and witty and angry songs.'

In recent years musicals have become a way of life for Jonathan Pryce, once hailed as the most brilliant Hamlet of his generation. After his award-winning performance as the Engineer in *Miss Saigon*, and his deliciously sinister Fagin in *Oliver!*, he's relishing playing the extrovert Henry Higgins in Trevor Nunn's production of *My Fair Lady*.

As we talk before opening night, it emerges that he's no newcomer to the great musical, famously based on Shaw's *Pygmalion*. Four years ago he took part in a concert version at the Hollywood Bowl before an audience of 18,000 people, with Lesley Garrett singing Eliza Doolittle. 'That was when I fell in love with the music and realised the great potential of the part,' he says. A word in impresario Cameron Mackintosh's ear led eventually to the National's production, in which Martine McCutcheon co-stars as Eliza. It was the quality of the songs that particularly attracted him. 'I like the fact they're dramatic and narrative, not just decorative. I think Lerner has dissected the play very skilfully. In the songs he gives you information which the play doesn't contain, using Shaw's epilogue. The lyrics are wonderful, nothing is wasted. He's done a fantastic job.'

Music has been a feature of Pryce's life since childhood. Brought up in north Wales, he was a boy soprano and sang in eisteddfods. ('I got a few green and white ribbons, but never the red one.') He gained his first job after RADA partly because he could sing, and he often had to use his voice in productions at the Liverpool Everyman. But it was a rendering of 'Witchcraft', at an informal cabaret after the first night of *Macbeth* at Stratford, that prompted his agent to suggest he get into musicals. Music has also taken over his screen career: in the forthcoming film *Unconditional Love* he plays a singer ('I'm a lounge act with a full head of hair, glitter suits and ten songs'). Yet like many actors he's only comfortable singing if he's playing a part. 'I find it very difficult to get up and sing just as me,' he admits. 'That's when all the nerves and fears and insecurities come back. But if I can hide behind a character, I love it.'

All this musical work, plus several major film roles, has kept him away from straight theatre since he played Astrov in *Uncle Vanya* as long ago as 1988. 'There have been plays I wanted to do, but they've never fitted in with other work. I'd like to do more eventually, but since *Miss Saigon* I've really enjoyed the big experience.' *My Fair Lady* certainly fits that category, and creating the role of Higgins has clearly been challenging but rewarding. 'It's an attractive part for an actor because of the range of emotions he goes through. He's obviously a brute, but a brute who goes on a journey, during which he shows people a more vulnerable side. It's very well crafted, the way he develops. I've played Petruchio in *The Taming of the Shrew*, another man who bullies a woman into submission, and I find there are parallels between the two characters.'

Are there, I wonder, aspects of Higgins in himself that he's been able to make use of? 'It's difficult to know what you're drawing from, especially while you're still rehearsing,' he says warily. 'And there's a side of me that doesn't want to divulge too much of that. I do think too much is written about performance: the more you talk about these things, the less there is for the audience to find out.' He very much approves of Nunn's directing style. 'I told him I like working *with* directors, not *for* them, and that's what's happening. He's a great director of large shows like *My Fair Lady*, he has a very good overall vision, while allowing you to get on with your own work.' And working with choreographer Matthew Bourne? 'I like dancing and I can put one foot in front of the other.'

There's a nice irony in the fact that such a quintessentially English character as Higgins, written by an Irishman, is now being played by a Welshman. 'I've been struggling with my Welsh accent,' Pryce confesses. 'My problem is my vowels: I say grass, as in ass, instead of grarse, so it's a learning curve. But I've played kings before now, so I'll probably get by.'

My Fair Lady opened in the Lyttelton in March 2001.

Not so much a photograph

Michael Morpurgo looks forward to the staging of his remarkable novel *War Horse*

Living on a farm in Devon, Michael Morpurgo knows a thing or two about horses. 'My wife and daughter love them, so they've been around a lot in my life. I've looked them in the eyes and seen a sensibility there, as well as a stupidity. They seem to have a kind of understanding of the person they are with.'

This knowledge and sympathy clearly proved invaluable when he came to write *War Horse*, his highly original and moving novel about the First World War, seen through the eyes of a horse. Published a quarter of a century ago, it's now getting the full stage treatment at the National, following in the footsteps of the hugely successful adaptations of Jamila Gavin's *Coram Boy* and Philip Pullman's *His Dark Materials*.

The inspiration for his novel was a 1917 drawing from the *Illustrated London News*, one of several left to his family by Allen Lane, the founder of Penguin Books. It depicted the British cavalry charging up a hill, with horses impaled on the barbed wire placed in front of the German infantry. 'It was a very powerful image,' he recalls. 'So I rang the Imperial War Museum to ask how many horses were lost in the war. They estimated two million on the British side alone. The waste was incredible. Yet most of them didn't die in battle; they were just ground down by the appalling conditions.'

In *War Horse*, one of the hundred books he has written, he focuses almost exclusively on life on the battlefields in France, where Joey the horse undergoes many trials and tribulations, serving on both sides, straying into no-man's-land, and sharing both the suffering and the comradeship of the ordinary soldiers. In telling this remarkable story, Morpurgo powerfully conveys the bitter experience of those terrible four years of carnage and attrition.

For the stage version, to be co-directed by Marianne Elliott and Tom Morris, the playwright Nick Stafford has further developed the human characters, who in the novel are only seen from Joey's perspective. They include the family on whose farm Joey was raised, as well as several soldiers of different ranks, both British and German, whom he encounters in the war zone.

With several weeks before rehearsals begin, how does Morpurgo view the transformation of his story? 'Putting it on the stage is taking it off in another direction and that's great. My problem is that I find it difficult to imagine how the script will work there. There's a lot of deviation from the novel, so I just have to go with that and enjoy what has been done dramatically. It's not like taking a photograph of the original, it's more like doing a painting from it. Some adaptations look just like that; but I want people to take liberties.'

Since his initial discussions with Stafford he has been to workshops at the National and talked about the script with Morris. His main comments have been on the scenes involving the farming family and the dialogue among the soldiers. 'I know about the agriculture of the period,' he says. 'I'm a country boy, I live among fields and hens and horses, and its nature hasn't changed much. I was also in the army, so I know how privates speak to officers, and officers to privates.'

Clearly, the major challenge for the National was how to give dramatic form to Joey and the other horses. Early on Morris came up with the solution: to get the actors to work with life-sized puppets, created by the internationally renowned Handspring Puppet Company. With rehearsals still some four months away, Morpurgo has yet to see these creations in action: 'But I have no doubt the results will be amazing.'

This is quite a year in the theatre for the former Children's Laureate, with stage adaptations of his works by the Birmingham Stage Company (*Kensuke's Kingdom*), the Unicorn (*Billy the Kid*) and the Bristol Old Vic (*The Mozart Question*). Yet success doesn't seem to have diminished his excitement about the process. 'I can't tell you how wonderful it is to have a story you have written on paper come to life in this way. It's a magical moment for an author.'

War Horse opened in the Olivier in October 2007.

Making *Waves*

Katie Mitchell explains her early thoughts about playing with Virginia Woolf's novel

I read Virginia Woolf's work at Oxford, and for this production I actually worked from the edition I had there. It's got my black biro marks in very strange places. I did a special paper on Woolf for my finals, so I read absolutely everything. I'm not sure I fully understood it, or that even now I understand all of it, but I do love it.

A lot of writers suffer hugely when they've got that blank piece of paper in front of them. But formally she was pushing the novel forward in a very brave and challenging way, and I think that might have caused her more torment than when she was writing other pieces. Her earlier works were closer to a novel as we would normally understand that. This isn't like that – it's just thoughts and voices, and you have to search for the story.

I chose *The Waves* because if I'd taken another novel, like *Mrs Dalloway* or *To the Lighthouse*, they're closer to a conventional novel. I don't think they would have posed as many challenges as this piece does. This is closer to theatre, because it's a series of what she calls dramatic monologues. I felt the absence of all the trappings of a normal novel, which are almost impossible to do on stage, might mean that we could make a live performance out of this material better than with one of the other novels. We would be inside people's heads, and that would be easier to do than the full landscape of six people's lives from the 1890s to the 1930s. If we were looking at the real world, we'd be very busy.

As a result of a workshop, we changed from using Bernard's summing-up, because we realised that the novel was written in the present tense and, if we did it as a flashback filtered through one person's mind, we would have constant tensions between the language that they're using and the concept. So we cut the final chapter, and we will do it from the beginning until their final meal at Hampton Court, which will make it more linear. We're using video and sound to create the evening, so we're not making any attempt at representing in scenes the action of the novel. So now there is a draft script. I cut the novel to forty pages, because we should only be doing one hour forty-five maximum. That was what the actors used in the workshop.

I'm nervous about what I might say today on the first day of rehearsals, because we might get halfway through rehearsals and realise we need to take it in a slightly different direction. If I planned it too literally and too concretely now, it might bear no relationship to the outcome. But I decided it wasn't possible to represent six people's lives in a series of lifelike scenes stretching from 1890 to 1930 without having a mammoth budget and a mammoth cast, who have to age, starting as children and being old by the end of it. If we did it cheaper, it could be quite naff, with a lot of quick changes and fragments of scenery. So I felt we needed to capture the essence of the writing in a completely different way.

Sound seemed to be a really useful way of thinking about the material, so we studied how radio uses sound and tried doing it like a radio piece. We then studied how Foley artists match human sounds to images, and realised if we were careful we could use images, images that we could construct live: so, for example, we can do a close-up on an eye and put some leaves around it, and it looks like a child's eye looking through a hedge, because our eyes don't grow, they stay the same size from birth to death. And then we realised that we could shoot faces when the age of the characters hit those of the actors.

We realised we could catch fragments of it through video and work predominantly with voice-over, that we could put together an exciting evening that would probably bring you closer to the novel than a normal theatrical representation would. A lot is left to the audience's imagination, as it is when you read a novel – you know how it is, you watch *Pride and Prejudice* on television and you think, 'That's not what it is!' Of course it isn't, because you have imagined it all in your head, you've made your own film as you read it. So it seemed better to pull back on representation, in order to allow the audience to make their own film from the fragments that we're giving them, or the oral cues or stimuli, that would be closer to the act of reading a novel.

It's more like a film script: the place is put down and then what's said there, because it's very hard when you read the novel to locate the place and the year the scenes are set in. So it's totally chronological, consisting of bits of every part of the novel, sometimes big, sometimes less so. We're drawing up ideas carried by Rhoda and Bernard, because their ideas are more dense and interesting, of story, of identity. Rhoda was always on the edge of a nervous breakdown and tends to have perceptions of the world that are more extraordinary than others'.

From here on I think the text will stay quite stable, but the shape of it might change. We can't do the filming of the waves on super-8 or 16-mil, so we're going to have to find another solution. We might have that one pre-recorded element, where you sit and watch the sea in silence at different times of day, which is very beautiful. But we might not be able to achieve that financially, as it's a very high-tech show.

You'll see the video elements being constructed and produced at the same time. So you'll see them shooting it: all the material is live except for the pictures of the sea. You'll see someone standing there with a camera pointing at someone's eye, someone else holding a bit of hedge and moving it, and someone else speaking a voice-over, and then four other people doing Foley sound effects. So it will be like a big screen and fragments, and that will close, and then there will be radio, then back to image. Quick changes as in *Dream Play* are not possible, and it puts too much strain on the organisation to do theatre that way. It nudges us in a different direction. I didn't want to repeat *Dream Play* formally, so we have headed in a different direction.

Waves opened in the Cottesloe in November 2006.

Brodie's head revisited

Phyllida Lloyd and Fiona Shaw discuss their
stage version of Muriel Spark's celebrated novel

'In a school structure that was boringly soviet in its attitude to
children, she came into the classroom like a shaft of anarchy.'
Like so many of us, Fiona Shaw has a particular figure lodged
in her memory of school, an inspirational, colourful, stimulating teacher who stood out from the rest. It's a memory she's
drawing on as she tackles the title role of *The Prime of Miss Jean
Brodie*, the stage adaptation of Muriel Spark's best-known
novel, which is about to be revived by the National.

It is, of course, a gorgeous role, that of the subversive radical
teacher fighting against the ethos of the 'team spirit' in 1930s
Edinburgh, who determines to make her pupils 'la crème de la
crème', and insists that Art, Truth and Beauty are of infinitely
more value to 'my girls' than such humdrum subjects as
science and mathematics. But this is no ordinary revival. With
Muriel Spark's blessing, Fiona Shaw and director Phyllida
Lloyd are working with the play's original adapter, Jay Presson
Allen, to produce a new version of the play that they hope will
be more in tune with our times, drawing on 'missing' material
from the novel and even, though to a lesser extent, on the
novelist's autobiography. 'Like translations, adaptations of
novels date very quickly,' Lloyd says. 'They suggest a
production style. The novel now feels more modern than the
adaptation. We need to revisit it.'

The novel, brilliantly economical and full of subtle time-
shifts, is certainly more complex than the play. It contains
several surprises, such as a scene depicting poverty in the Old
Town and many acute observations from the narrator, who at
one point describes Miss Brodie as 'an Edinburgh Festival all
on her own'. One element Shaw and Lloyd are keen to include
in the play is Miss Brodie's pluralist religious outlook against a
background of stern Scottish Presbyterianism. Shaw also
suggests: 'We want to show the excitement and unusualness of
somebody who went on learning throughout her life rather

than stopping at twenty, and the wonderful battle that is waged between bohemian and suburban values.' They've also made use of Muriel Spark's portrait of Miss Kay, the teacher from her schooldays who provided the model for Jean Brodie. 'She had a profound influence on her life and was clearly someone who exploded the imagination of all the children around her,' Lloyd explains.

Director and actor recently worked with a group of drama students from Queen Mary College in Edinburgh, 'performing' the entire novel over a couple of days, and getting the girls to do imaginative exercises based on scenes omitted from the play. 'We found it quite Chekhovian in places, elegiac and haunting,' Lloyd recalls. They produced a list of possible rewrites for Jay Presson Allen to work on. While not playing down the darker side of Jean Brodie's character – her absurd lack of self-criticism, her manipulativeness, her flirtation with fascism – they do want to shift the picture from that of a slightly eccentric schoolteacher to the more radical visionary.

Lloyd touches on a further point she feels may be overlooked in the play: 'We realised that at that time female teachers could not be married, so women were making a real sacrifice by going into teaching, dedicating themselves to a life of virginity, almost like a priesthood.' Both she and Shaw believe the play chimes in with the current debate about what should be taught in schools. Lloyd observes: 'It's the national curriculum versus the unpackagable alternative, the question of whether you can plan education in advance, or allow for imaginative responses to individual children.'

Significantly, in her autobiography Muriel Spark applies to Miss Kay her fellow writer John Steinbeck's belief that 'a great teacher is a great artist, and that there are as few as there are any other great artists'. He suggested that 'teaching might even be the greatest of the arts, since the medium is the human mind and spirit'.

The Prime of Miss Jean Brodie opened in the Lyttelton in June 1998.

Collective effort

Simon McBurney talks about the latest show from his ground-breaking company Complicite

'Every show is a shot in the dark,' Simon McBurney admits. 'Some succeed, some don't; but they all try to do something different.' The artistic director of Complicite is finding it difficult to talk about the company's forthcoming show at the National. But that's mainly because, six months before opening night, it's still in the process of being created. What he can be sure of is that it will be a musical piece based on the work of the 1930s Soviet surrealist writer Daniil Kharms, who was liquidated by Stalin in 1942. 'That's the starting point – but God knows what the finishing point will be.'

Most Complicite shows – the 1991 National production of Dürrenmatt's *The Visit* was a rare exception – are devised by members of the company. They spend several months researching an idea, then developing, testing and extending it in rehearsal. Each show is different from the previous one, underlining McBurney's belief that 'the spirit of inquiry is the only thing that keeps the theatre alive'. So what drew him to an obscure writer such as Kharms? 'I suppose it was something to do with the symbolic nature of his story,' he says. 'He was a comic, crazy man, very much in the tradition of the holy fool. He belonged to a group that made up all kinds of nonsensical ideas about what art is. His writing is very poignant and funny, almost like slapstick, and I think it's possible through his work to say something about our society.'

Complicite is often marked down as a group specialising in physical theatre. McBurney dislikes such a label, seeing it as restrictive. 'There is no one Complicite style,' he insists. 'All theatre is physical: we're imprisoned in our bodies, so we have to express ourselves through our bodies. It's just that in English theatre the physical element has atrophied and almost disappeared.' Like many who have joined the company that he and three others founded eleven years ago, he trained in Paris with Jacques Lecoq, a teacher whose influence on a younger generation of British actors has been considerable. But he disagrees with the distinction usually made between theatre in the UK and the rest of Europe. 'I don't see any difference between British and Continental styles,' he says. 'I just see it all as theatre. The ability to communicate is what counts, so vocal and physical skills are equally crucial. I don't like the categorisation of styles, or one group being set up against another. I admire most people's work at some level.'

Although he's the director, he stresses that the shows are very much a collective effort, drawing on the imaginations of all the actors. 'I have an enormous belief in the power of people's creativity,' he says. 'Although I provide the outside eye, I treat the actors as intelligent beings, and we experiment and try things out together.' A couple of days spent recently working with Peter Brook focused his thoughts on what makes a piece of improvisation come alive. 'You don't always know how it works, there are deeper instincts involved,' he says. 'It has nothing to do with whether it's naturalistic or not, it's to do with the way the audience can focus on what's going on.'

He emphasises Complicite's aim of providing popular theatre that will have an appeal beyond the traditional middle-class audience. Indeed, he believes an over-intellectual approach to its work by critics and others can result in confusion. 'The perception of ordinary audiences is often very different from that of the experts, who can get between the people and the work,' he says. 'The experts come up afterwards and say "What's the story?" Ordinary people say, "It made me cry, but I don't know why."'

The company tries to reach as many different groups as possible through its workshops, which it sees as important to the development of a show. It has done a lot of education work with young people, including many with special needs. 'When we're on tour, we try to liberate people's enjoyment of theatre,' McBurney says. 'In the early days we worked with handicapped kids and got some fantastic results. But most kids love our way of working; they see it as a kind of game.'

Complicite's last production at the National, *The Street of Crocodiles*, won glowing reviews. That show too was based on the work of a little-known writer, Bruno Schulz. But there, we can assume, any resemblance to the forthcoming production will end.

Out of a House Walked a Man opened in the Lyttelton in December 1994.

North is north

Ayub Khan-Din talks about the background to *Rafta, Rafta . . .*

Back in the 1970s in Salford, Ayub Khan-Din and his family used to watch the BBC weekend film matinées on television. One of his favourites was *The Family Way*, based on Bill Naughton's play *All in Good Time*. 'I loved that film, I remember the feeling I had watching it and how I always cried at the end,' he says. 'So when I came to write *Rafta, Rafta . . .* my aim was to take the audience through a similar experience, to press the same buttons.'

His very funny yet poignant adaptation of Naughton's play has been warmly received by the critics and has been delighting audiences in the Lyttelton. 'I wanted to show an ordinary working-class Asian family, who are very integrated and fairly happy, with no major problems except for this friction between father and son,' he explains. 'I just wanted to give people a great evening in the theatre.'

Unable to afford a home of their own, the son and his new wife are forced to live with his parents, a proximity that prevents them from consummating their marriage. It's a situation which Khan-Din believes is a common one: 'It's not just an Asian thing, it's universal what these characters are going through. In the 1970s young couples could afford their own house, but now it's very hard to get on the property ladder.'

His own climb up the theatrical ladder is an inspiring one. At school he was, by his own admission, a hopelessly late developer, who didn't read until he was nine. As a teenager he went with a friend to a couple of youth theatres, but was too embarrassed to go alone when his friend dropped out. He worked for a while as a hairdresser ('my parents wouldn't let me sign on the dole') before suddenly deciding to become an actor. With only a couple of CSEs to his name, he scraped on to a drama course at Salford Tech, then did three years at Mountview Theatre School.

It was there that he lost his accent: 'Someone said to me, "If you want to run with the wolves, you've got to learn to howl like them."' Before long he was appearing in films, most notably *My Beautiful Launderette* and *Sammy and Rosie Get Laid*. But he had been writing since his days at drama school, and in 1996 he scored a huge hit with his play *East is East*, filmed three years later. In it he drew on his own family, which consisted of seven brothers, two sisters, a Muslim father and a British mother.

Rafta, Rafta . . . too has strong autobiographical elements. 'I have this thing about father–son relationships,' he says. 'My father was an illiterate villager from Kashmir, who came to England in 1930 and moved up a notch. As a child I watched how his relationship with all his other sons deteriorated. I never had that problem myself, perhaps because I went to Pakistan when I was twelve and later got into college, which he was really impressed about, and then to drama school, which he still insists, whatever I say, on calling a university.'

He dislikes being described as an Asian playwright, and is irritated that because he's half-Pakistani he's often asked to write something about suicide bombers. 'I am Asian, that's a fact, but I don't like the way it's used to pigeonhole a writer. I'm a playwright first and foremost. Although my ethnicity at times informs my work, it isn't all of it.' As it happens his next play, set in Salford, is about a white family.

Meanwhile he's optimistic about the progress made towards a genuinely multicultural theatre. 'I'll probably be shot down in flames for saying it, but I think it's really healthy at the moment. It's completely different from when I left drama school and joined Tara Arts. Then there were separate entities.

But gradually more and more rep companies tried to get involved with their Asian audiences. They started to hire black and Asian directors, and use integrated casting. But it's been a very long process.'

Rafta, Rafta . . . is clearly another positive step in that process, with multicultural audiences coming to the National to see a play featuring the Bollywood star Harish Patel and the multi-talented Meera Syal, now part of mainstream British culture.

Rafta, Rafta . . . opened in the Lyttelton in April 2007.

Another inspector calls

David Farr on his modern version of Gogol's classic comedy *The Government Inspector*

June seems set to be a hectic month for David Farr. After successful spells as artistic director of the Gate and joint artistic director of the Bristol Old Vic, he's moving into the top job at the Lyric Hammersmith. At the same time his play *The UN Inspector*, a version of Nikolai Gogol's great comedy, which he's directing himself, will be opening at the National.

It's not the first time this busy playwright and director has plundered Russian literature for dramatic purposes. Three years ago his reworking of Dostoevsky's famous novel resulted in *Crime and Punishment in Dalston*. The play caught the attention of the National's director Nicholas Hytner, who suggested he do something similar with Gogol's *The Government Inspector*. 'I've tried to take Gogol's essential view of the world, which is cruelly black and farcical, and apply it to today,' he says. 'So much has changed since he wrote it. We've had Czarist Russia, the Bolshevik revolution and the fall of communism. But the issues and tensions remain very much the same, although the economic forces are bigger now.'

Gogol's satirical comedy, first performed in St Petersburg in 1836, paints a damning picture of municipal corruption. 'I decided to collect into one heap everything I then knew about what was bad in Russia,' Gogol wrote, 'and laugh at the whole lot in one go.' The story revolves around the arrival in a Russian village of a penniless clerk, who is mistaken for a government inspector. Hailed by the progressives as a manifesto for social reform, the play prompted howls of protest from the reactionaries, who called it a libel on Russia and demanded that Gogol, who was Ukrainian, be sent to Siberia. It only escaped censorship because Czar Nicholas I demanded to see it. 'Well, what a play!' he observed afterwards. 'Everybody caught it, most of all me.'

The UN Inspector is set in an unnamed former Soviet Union country, and the 'inspector' – actually an estate agent and a complete nobody – comes from England. It's an entertaining mixture of satire and farce, in which a bunch of corrupt and hypocritical national politicians are rudely unmasked, and the man from Foxton's unwittingly stirs up revolutionary unrest among the people. 'Gogol was a nationalist writer, even a mystical writer in a way,' Farr observes. 'He saw the potential of this great land being frustrated by corruption and injustice, and longed for a better world. He was interested in the soul of Russia, whereas my version is about global politics – the soul of the world, if you like.'

It's noticeable how close he has kept the text to the structure and dialogue patterns of the original. Did he feel Gogol looking over his shoulder? 'Not at all – though I've read a lot of him and I love his work. I just don't see the point of changing the play structurally, it would cease to be the same if you took it out of those two rooms. It also has the unity of time within the scenes: it's much more fun if you can contain the action within the classical unities. That's essential if you want to tame the chaos.' He has, however, introduced two new characters, a finance minister and an investigative journalist, and changed the status of others – for example, the wife of the president (Gogol's town prefect) is now a more powerful figure. 'As I worked on the play I allowed some of the characters to move away from the original, so there are now different kinds of archetypes.'

Farr's success as a writer – he's had plays at the RSC, the Bush and the Young Vic, and has just been commissioned by the National to do a version of Kafka's *The Trial* – has run in parallel to a substantial directing career. This began at school, where he was part of a group that borrowed the school gym to direct themselves in plays. At university he formed a company with two actresses, calling themselves the Talking Tongues, and staging devised two-handers in basement discos and other small spaces. One piece won the *Guardian* Student Drama Award at the Edinburgh Festival, and he was on his way.

The UN Inspector will be the eighth of his plays that he's also directed. There was apparently never any question of someone else being offered the job. 'Because it's an adaptation I think it will be possible to keep a little more of a distance, which is good. I'm also working with my usual team, designer Ti Green and composer Keith Clouston, and that will help.' But he agrees this dual role can have drawbacks as well as advantages. 'In the early weeks in rehearsal your role as a writer is to make sure the text is working, even if you can see that the actors aren't quite there yet. If you're directing as well, you have less time to keep an eye on that. On the other hand, if you have actors who trust you enough to say that some speech isn't working, then you can work out what to do and change it very quickly. Of course, it's tough to be completely objective, but you have to try.'

The UN Inspector opened in the Olivier in June 2005.

Fighting a memory

Desmond Barrit on following a comic legend in
*A Funny Thing Happened on the Way to the
Forum*

If you ask an actor what he wants to do, he'll say a bit of Shakespeare on Monday, a musical on Tuesday, a TV on Wednesday, a radio play on Thursday, an advert that pays you a lot of money on Friday, and the weekend to yourself. But you can't choose. My criterion is whether a job excites me, and *A Funny Thing Happened on the Way to the Forum* really does. But I have a problem. When this Sondheim musical was staged in London twenty years ago, Pseudolus was played by Frankie Howerd. Even today I can still hear him saying every line. So although there's no way I'm going to totally forget his voice, in playing the part I've got to fight against that memory, try to unhear him and make the part my own.

I love musicals. There's nothing more exciting than being behind a curtain and hearing the overture. The last one I did was *My Fair Lady*, a concert performance in the Hollywood Bowl, with Jonathan Pryce, Lesley Garrett and myself. When the 140-piece orchestra started playing I burst into tears: the sheer volume of sound was the most exciting thing I'd ever heard. My voice is a low baritone. When people say, 'What's your range?' I say, 'I've no idea, I'll sing for you and we'll see.' Frankie Howerd and Zero Mostel, who played Pseudolus in America, didn't really have voices, so it's not being immodest to say mine is hugely better than theirs. If you're in the chorus in a musical, you have to sing properly, but principals can get away with blue murder. As long as I've got thirty people singing behind me, I sound fantastic: it's as if Gigli has been dug up and is singing on stage again.

I didn't start acting until I was thirty-two and I did pantomime for six or seven years. I had no formal training, I just learnt by watching people. Panto is a good training for *Forum*, because talking to the audience is what it's all about, it gives you lots of opportunities to break down the fourth wall. Actors have a fear of looking at the audience. But if you look an individual directly in the eye and say, 'Were you laughing?' they smile and chuckle. Then the people around them have the impression you're talking to *them* and it spreads. Even though people pretend to be embarrassed, they love being dragged into the action, being spoken to and asked their opinion.

I think comedic acting demands a much more technical approach than dramatic acting. You have to superimpose the reality on top of it, because people won't laugh unless they think you're being sincere. Sadly, not so much validation is given to comedic acting: proper actors do Hamlet, non-proper ones do Bottom. I don't know where I fit in. Adrian Noble said I was the Royal Shakespeare Company's answer to light entertainment. With a face like mine, doing comedy is the obvious thing. But like all comedic actors I really want to do stuff that tugs at people's heartstrings. I've enjoyed tremendously playing Falstaff, and Eddie Carbone in *A View from the Bridge*, and Malvolio, who is a tragi-comic character. But *Forum* is a great opportunity to go out there and just have a bloody marvellous time.

A Funny Thing Happened on the Way to the Forum opened in the Olivier in July 2004.

Following their passions

Kneehigh Theatre brings a famous love story from Cornwall to the Cottesloe

It's been described by the poet Charles Causley as Cornwall's National Theatre. It began in 1980, when actor and teacher Mike Shepherd started to run workshops for an eclectic group of individuals. These quickly turned into performances, with stories being told in a wild and anarchic spirit in a variety of venues, many of them outdoors.

Today Kneehigh is recognised as one of the most energetic and original theatre companies around.

Its roots are in the rugged Cornish landscape, full of wild beauty but until recently empty of theatres. Starting in village halls, the company has performed on clifftops and harbour sides, in preaching pits, quarries, gunpowder works, barns, woods, castles, even car parks. Its productions are praised for their vigorous imagination and visual flair, and their skill in mixing comedy and tragedy. Yet its shows are not confined to county matters.

'We make theatre in, for and inspired by Cornwall,' says

director Emma Rice. 'The artist Joán Miró once said that to be truly universal you must be truly local. That could be our company manifesto. But we're not here to further the cause of Cornwall, because that kind of boundary becomes inhibiting. In choosing which stories to tell we follow the desires and passions of individuals in the company.' Kneehigh delights in playing to mixed audiences, which can range from age eight to eighty. During a performance of *The Bacchae* at the Lyric Hammersmith I watched the actors well and truly put the rip into Euripides, delighting a predominantly teenage audience with a pantomime-style first half, then stunning them into fascinated silence with a visually arresting climax to the grisly Greek tragedy.

Another recent production was an award-winning take on Hans Christian Andersen's fairy tale *Red Shoes*, which won over audiences from Beijing to Battersea. The way the shows are created is unusual. Rice puts together a palette of ideas: design, music, text and dance are all ingredients in the devising mix. 'The material hasn't yet been formed into a structure,' she explains. 'We wait to see what happens when we put it into the crucible and give the characters to the actors. I don't want the writer to create the characters, I want the actor and the writer and myself to do so together. We write on the hoof and do a lot of structuring as we go along.'

The group spirit is clearly reinforced by the conditions in which the company works. Its rehearsal space, which has no heating, is near Mevagissey in the small fishing village of Gorran Haven, which has no eating places. So each rehearsal day begins with a run up the cliffs to get warm, while all meals are cooked communally.

It seems surprising that Kneehigh has only now got round to that famous story of love, revenge and betrayal *Tristan & Yseult*, since it is Cornwall's oldest love story and commemorated locally: on the roadside on the way to Fowey stands a stone bearing a sixth-century Latin inscription, which translates as 'Here lies Tristan the son of King Mark of Cornwall'. 'It's been waiting in the wings for a long time,' Emma Rice admits. 'I struggled with it for a while, wondering how to reinvent it. Then I got interested in the marginal character of the woman Tristan eventually marries, who's also called Yseult. They never had sex, he was not in love with her. This led to the idea of telling the story through a Chorus of the Unloved, so that within this beautiful love story we see the pain and the human loss that happens in all great love affairs.'

Tristan & Yseult has already been staged out of doors, among other places at the Eden Project and the famous Minack Theatre in Cornwall. Now the challenge is to adapt it for the National and its audience. 'At first we thought we would simply distil the existing show for indoors,' Emma Rice says. 'But after experiencing the intimate atmosphere of the Cottesloe, I felt we should reconceive it for an urban space.'

Tristan & Yseult opened in the Cottesloe in April 2005.

The joy of illusion

Phelim McDermott reveals why Improbable Theatre is tackling a famous horror film

Theatre of Blood is one of those wonderfully crappy cult films that everyone remembers. It's camp and fantastic, it's got Vincent Price playing the old-style actor Lionheart, it has a host of wonderful British character actors to die for, and it's a horror film about actors and critics. What more could you ask for?

I've often thought it would be great to do it as a theatre show. The story is partly about what is good and bad acting, and that's a question I ask myself a lot. Often I enjoy shows where the acting is not so good, or where the set's a bit wobbly or very obviously painted. You'd think such things would make it harder to suspend your disbelief, but it can have the opposite effect. The audience knows you're pretending, and can let go and really believe. Film is a single image, which says, 'This is the reality you're watching.' Theatre is a series of layers: it's the thing you're watching, the imagination of the audience, plus the audience imagining what's going on in the head of the actor.

Initially Lee Simpson and I wanted to do our version in an old theatre, but Nicholas Hytner persuaded us to play it in the Lyttelton. Then we realised that the film was made at the time when the National was being built and, when it was complete, Laurence Olivier would hand over the directorship to Peter Hall. This seemed to contain an echo of our story, in which an old-style actor-manager finds that the world of theatre has changed and there is no longer a place for him. We also wanted to get away from it just being a story about bumping off the critics.

In our version Shakespeare is a much bigger element: Lionheart speaks almost nothing but speeches from the plays. While the film darts all over the place, we make the setting more like Prospero's island: the critics are all invited to the theatre, though for different reasons. One of them is tempted by an assignation, another comes about a possible job as literary manager for the new National on the South Bank.

In some ways the footage of the old Shakespearean actors at the start of the film is the most exciting part of it. The style is actually very shocking, but also very beautiful. I've always had an interest in old-style acting – *Shockheaded Peter* was a bit of a celebration of it – and our shows have always had a lot of obviously theatrical elements. People come to the theatre to see what theatre does best: this show is a celebration of that, of the mechanics and joy of illusion, of theatricality.

We've been asked if we're staging the story because we hate the critics. Actually we're not doing any specific portraits of today's bunch, so it will be up to them to decide whether they can spot elements of themselves. They may be upset if they do – but also if they don't. In fact, they have been pretty kind to Improbable over the years, so we don't have a beef about them. I also think they are important. If you have an opinion from the outside, the so-called enemy becomes tangible and it can help crystallise the company's vision or intention. Of course, you can defend yourself against the criticism, or the truly awake can find out what's right about it, even if that's only a small element. You know it wouldn't bother us if some part of us didn't believe the criticism in some way ourselves.

We've debated whether Lionheart is a good or bad actor. I think he should sometimes look like the best you've ever seen and sometimes the worst, probably at the same moment. It's a part where one has to have self-awareness, to be able to embrace that bit of oneself that wants to be the greatest actor in the world, but also to have the ability to laugh at that ambition. Jim Broadbent has both elements. He's also an incredibly funny man, who has the potential to be very scary. That's a unique combination.

Theatre of Blood opened in the Lyttelton in April 2005.

From page to stage

Helen Edmundson looks at the challenge of adapting Tolstoy's *War and Peace* for the theatre

After adapting *Anna Karenina*, it seems brave to take on *War and Peace*. Yet this is precisely what Helen Edmundson has done for Shared Experience, whose production of her adaptation of Tolstoy's great historical novel comes to the National in the summer.

'I like to work on books that grapple with life and death, where the themes are huge and epic,' she says. 'I also think that Tolstoy has such wisdom to offer on the human condition. But this is definitely the most difficult book I've had to work on.' A playwright herself, her previous adaptations have included George Eliot's *The Mill on the Floss* and *Anna Karenina* – both wonderfully inventive and much-admired productions for Shared Experience – as well as Alexandre Dumas' *The Corsican Brothers*.

'The problem with *War and Peace* is that, unlike *Anna Karenina*, it's not a psychological novel,' she explains. 'This makes it very difficult to turn a character inside out and to physicalise their problems in theatrical terms.' Another major challenge has been Tolstoy's view of historical events and characters. 'He was very good on facts, but quite biased in his interpretation of them,' she suggests. 'So you have to decide whether you're going to correct his bias, as for instance in the hatchet job he did on Napoleon.'

In this respect she was greatly helped by two research trips to Russia, during which she was able to visit the Tolstoy Museum, his town house and his country estate at Yasnaya Polyana, and meet up with several Russian academics. 'It was very good to get to grips with the Russian psyche, it does help you to understand their fatalism,' she recalls. 'But I found there were many different interpretations of the historical parts of the book – which was great, because it meant that I could decide on the one that appealed to me most.'

Getting the right balance between being faithful to the author's intentions and creating a vibrant piece of theatre is evidently no easy matter. Often it's a question of finding a device that will provide a fresh angle on the story. In the case of *Anna Karenina* she had Anna and Levin, who hardly meet in the novel, talking to each other in limbo, acting as each other's sounding boards. In *The Mill on the Floss* she highlighted the idea of witch ducking to compensate for some of the structural defects of the novel and the anticlimax of the ending.

She believes it's essential for adaptors to be playwrights too, but she is critical of many (Mike Alfreds she thinks is an exception) for sticking too closely to the book. 'People think they can open the book and just use the dialogue as it is,' she observes. 'Hardy adaptations, for instance, are usually unbear-ably dull.' Working with a physically inventive company such as Shared Experience she finds liberating, because she knows ways will be found in rehearsal of losing chunks of text in favour of action or visual images. So she's looking forward to seeing how the company deals with the battle scenes and the burning of Moscow: 'Writing chaos can be very difficult,' she admits.

War and Peace opened in the Cottesloe in June 1996.

Jerry Springer from scratch

Richard Thomas and Stewart Lee recall the
evolution of their controversial hit opera

RICHARD THOMAS (*creator and composer*)   I think opera is a
very extreme medium, so you need extreme subjects. I was
watching *The Jerry Springer Show* on television one night and it
suddenly came to me: I was looking at eight people screaming
at each other and I couldn't understand a word they were
saying. It was opera! We first tried out the idea of *Jerry Springer
– The Opera* at a 'scratch night' at Battersea Arts Centre: you
meet the audience in the bar afterwards and they tell you what
they think. We then did the first half at the BAC Opera
Festival, developed it some more, and performed a concert
version at the Edinburgh Festival last summer.

STEWART LEE (*co-writer and director*)   Hundreds of people
gave us feedback while we were developing it and that was
really useful. All kinds of people loved it: some who had never
been to an opera or musical in their life, others who'd seen
opera, but didn't think it could be so funny.

RT   People refer to its mix of musical styles, but I don't really
believe in style. If you look at an eighties pop song you can see
the same kind of chord sequence as in Bach or Mozart.
Syncopation wasn't invented in the twentieth century, complex rhythms have always been around. Any echo of other
composers is unconscious: it's impossible to write a piece
without some hint or reference to the whole tone or blues scale.
You've just got your sonic canvas and all these amazing
colours. And I like to paint bright.

SL   I direct the whole play as it is in the score. All the timing
is in the music, because the rhythm of the language is so close
to the rhythm of the music. Also what's being said is often
opposite to the mood of the music. They work against each
other in a really great way, so you just have to go along with the
contrast, leave it alone, and not try to improve any reading or
get the actors to emote.

RT   I remember agonising over whether Jerry himself should sing, and if so whether he was a tenor or a baritone. But having him as the only speaking character provides a different rhythm and also gives the audience a bit of a rest. It's also a good way of solving the problem of how you jump from text to song and back to text.

SL   It's not a parody or a pastiche. And it's not a spoof of the TV show, or a satire on Jerry Springer. Nor is it an attack on his guests. In fact, people who've seen it say it elevates them to a kind of dignity.

RT   Jerry Springer came to see the show in Edinburgh and gave it a standing ovation. Audiences there were an interesting mix: we had grandparents bringing their grandchildren.

SL   Doing it at the National extends the joke. You take a stupid idea, you turn it into an opera – and now we're doing it in the temple of culture.

RT   Perhaps we should do it with just finger puppets?

Jerry Springer – The Opera opened in the Lyttelton in April 2003.

The sad revolutionary

Willis Hall, Keith Waterhouse and Tim Supple look forward to a production of *Billy Liar*

'I think the play's remained popular because we all have a bit of Billy in us. We all live inside our imaginations and have our own secret worlds.' Playwright Willis Hall saw the dramatic potential of Keith Waterhouse's novel *Billy Liar* the minute he read it back in 1959. 'It just leapt out at me that here was a stage play,' he recalls. Within a year the result of the two writers' collaboration was in the West End, with Albert Finney as Billy.

Since then the archetypal story of a young man's vain efforts to escape his northern upbringing has been made into a film, a TV series and a musical, while both the novel and the play have become set texts in schools. The play has been widely translated, or adapted: in Hugh Leonard's Irish version, for instance, Billy sets his sights on Dublin. There have been numerous professional and amateur productions – there's even talk of a New York production with a black Billy. 'It's always running somewhere,' Keith Waterhouse says.

Yet Tim Supple's new mobile production for the National will be the first to reach London since the original directed by Lindsay Anderson. So how is he approaching a play that now seems like a period piece, written when National Service was still compulsory, Harold Macmillan was Prime Minister, hula-hoops were all the rage and Cliff Richard had only just been invented? 'Because the play is about clichés, you have to work hard to avoid doing it in a clichéd way,' Supple says. 'But it's not a two-dimensional comedy, which is how it's sometimes played. Billy's father, for instance, is a sad, broken man. A good actor will get behind his clichéd words and show you his frustration at the impotence of his life.'

As a director, he believes the play has the power to appeal to a modern audience. 'It's a brilliantly articulated reproach of the philistinism of the time,' he says. 'But the hero can't articulate it himself, he's a not-quite-revolutionary and his revolution is pitiful. That's where the power of the story lies.'

The word 'nigger' in one speech by Billy's father has been changed to 'blackie'. 'It now sounds gratuitously offensive,' Waterhouse admits. Hall recalls that in their youth in Leeds there was only one black man in Hunslet, and when he went by children would stare at him in wonder. 'And every other black dog or cat was called Nigger: the overtones hadn't crossed the Atlantic,' he says.

Waterhouse stresses that, though he himself did work for an undertaker, his own family circumstances were very different from Billy's: he was one of five children brought up in a council house in Leeds and his father died when he was very young. But there are, he agrees, autobiographical elements in the story. 'Most young adults with any imagination were that way inclined, which is why it still strikes a chord, people recognise elements of themselves in Billy. They also recognise the conflict between generations – and that's not going to stop, is it?'

Billy Liar opened in the Cottesloe in December 1992.

Fairy tale with claws

Dragon combines the talents of Ultz, Spitting Image, M. C. Kinky, street entertainers and stand-up comics

'He wrote what seemed to be innocent stories for children, but they always had a political message.' On the eve of rehearsals for the National's latest family show, *Dragon* by Yevgeny Shvarts, its director and designer Ultz is reflecting on its creator and the play's chequered history.

Combining elements of Russian folklore with stinging satire, it was written and performed in 1943 in the middle of Stalin's tyrannical rule. It was banned after its first performance and not staged again until the mid-1960s – by which time its author was dead. How then did Shvarts escape Stalin's wrath, and continue to write his subversive plays and stories for several years? Ultz offers an explanation: 'A lot of his friends did mysteriously disappear. But Shvarts was popular around Leningrad, so it would be like trying to erase Lenny Henry: his absence would be noticed.'

The play is supposedly set in a small town in Scandinavia at the beginning of the nineteenth century. At one level it operates as a humorous, all-action entertainment for children, with the traditional ingredients of dragons, villains, a maiden in distress and a heroic knight – who is even called Lancelot. But it also works as a full-blooded political satire, of a society so bowed down by tyranny that, as one character puts it, 'even the ashtrays do what they're told'. The real sting comes in the second act: although the dragon has been slain by Lancelot, the Burgomaster rewrites history by claiming the deed as his, and the townspeople meekly swap one tyranny for another. As Lancelot says after giving them their freedom: 'The dragon must be slain in every one of you.'

Puppets play a key role in the play. Some of the characters are half-human, half-puppet, and on occasions even walls and windows become animated. So the National has brought in the expertise of Spitting Image to help crack some of the technical problems, and provide creative inspiration and technical know-how for the animatronics and the costumes that will hide the puppeteers. Roger Law, who runs Spitting Image, says: 'It's different from television. You're got to solve the problem of how the things will work night after night. We're bringing our knowledge, but the hard work is being done by the National's prop workshop. But it's not a Spitting Image show. If the kids come along thinking that, they'll be disappointed.'

For this new English version Ultz has added some extra ingredients. The gypsies, who stand for a type of alternative society, have their own reggae band and play music specially written for the show by M. C. Kinky. He's also included in the cast several actors who are street entertainers or stand-up comics in their own right. The play is subtitled 'A Fairy Tale with Claws', an apt description for a show that seems set to provide an exhilarating mix of humour, surprise, subversion and visual pyrotechnics. As Ultz puts it: 'It's not important for the audience to know about Stalinism, because it stands up as a fable in its own right. It can apply to any society.'

Dragon opened in the Olivier in November 1992.

Part Three

Actors and Directors
at Work

THE GREEKS AND SHAKESPEARE

Pulsating with conflict

Euripides' *Bacchai* is Peter Hall's latest foray into Greek tragedy

Peter Hall, who knows a thing or two about Greek theatre, is in no doubt about the stature of Euripides' masterpiece. 'I think it's one of the most original plays ever written and certainly in the top dozen of all time. Like Shakespeare's work, it's full of meaningful ambiguity and metaphorical significance. And whenever it's performed it seems to be extraordinarily timely.'

At a time when violence and revenge have become all too familiar concepts, his interpretation of this powerful tragedy seems likely to continue the tradition. Hall has assembled a top-notch team for his forthcoming production at the National: the new version is by playwright and classical scholar Colin Teevan, the music is being written by Harrison Birtwistle, and costume and set designs are by Alison Chitty.

One of Euripides' last two works, *Bacchai* has long been on Hall's list of plays he wants to direct. 'I've lived with it for over fifty years, seen it two or three times, but never been satisfied with it,' he says. 'The main problem is the portrayal of the erotic on stage. That seems to be extremely tricky, especially for the English. If you study the text, though, the erotic is portrayed off stage, along with the violence. The Greeks always left it to the imagination.'

Euripides' drama about the cult of Dionysus is concerned with elemental political, emotional and sexual forces, and is pulsating with conflict – between faith and instinct, reason and emotion, power and freedom, chaos and order, man and woman. The contradictions in the story are part of its appeal for Hall: 'What I like about the Greek mindset is that it can accept the idea that the opposite is also true. The problem with most philosophies and religions is that they can't accept that notion.'

Recently he spent a day in the university library in Houston, Texas, looking at more than thirty versions of *Bacchai*. 'It was like looking at thirty different plays,' he recalls. 'There were the late Victorians, Gilbert Murray, then the stripped and bare or overtly colloquial versions of the twentieth century. But Euripides was deliberately looking for a formal quality, which I think Colin has caught extremely well.'

As with his earlier productions of Greek tragedies at the National – Aeschylus' *The Oresteia* in 1981 and Sophocles' *The Oedipus Plays* in 1996 – the chorus and protagonists will be wearing full masks. Hall believes that Greek drama doesn't work without them: 'The mask allows you to explore the extremities of emotion and suffering and pain, and still be communicating, attractive and understandable.'

The company's experience is mixed: actors such as Greg Hicks and David Ryall are familiar with the mask, but others will be starting from scratch. Hall stresses that the initial encounter with the mask can be an unnerving, even intimidating, experience for an actor. So in rehearsals he'll initially be working separately on the text and improvising with the masks.

'Some people find the mask claustrophobic, while others find it too self-revealing, because it releases something in themselves they don't want to look at,' he explains. 'The process is always the same for those who come new to it. At first they're just thinking about their new identity and it takes them about a week to speak. After ten days they start to relate to each other, but become very hostile and belligerent, very territorial. Then gradually, after about three weeks, they become a collective. It's very mysterious and after a lifetime of work on masks, I still don't know why it happens.'

As he did for *The Oresteia*, Harrison Birtwistle will sit in on rehearsals during the day and at night write the music based on what he observes. 'I've worked with many talented people, but not with many geniuses,' Hall says. 'Harry is one; he's also a marvellous collaborator. His music is uniquely suited to this kind of play: it's harsh and barbaric, very rhythmic, sensual and essentially dramatic.'

Although he's not yet decided where to set the play – Afghanistan, Kosovo or London are all possibilities – he wants it to be a 'violently contemporary' production: 'We want to do it in some species of modern dress, so that it doesn't feel antiquy.' He's declined to meet the National's normal deadlines for costume and set designs, being quite prepared to end up 'with a bare Olivier stage and a lighting rig' rather than make crucial decisions in advance of rehearsals.

'I couldn't do it any other way. With proper theatre work, if you decide what a play is before you do it, if you decide on the route before the journey, you get nowhere. The play can only emerge from a process of work with the actors, the composer and the designer. You have to build it up as you go along.'

Bacchai opened in the Olivier in May 2002.

From do-wop to hip-hop

Fiona Laird is rehearsing an all-singing, all-dancing version of Aristophanes' *Frogs*

Standing together, arms folded in stage-housewife fashion, the two women suddenly spot Dionysus across the room. ''Ere, look, in't that 'im?' says one in broad Yorkshire tones. 'I'd recognise those boots anywhere, they're that poofy.' Eventually they flounce off, leaving director Fiona Laird chuckling with delight. 'That's it, that's really good. But remember you're almost two people joined together as one. So overlap with each other a bit more and make it more aggressive.'

It only needs a few minutes in this south London rehearsal room to make you realise the National's mobile touring production of this Greek comedy, mounted by NT

Education, is far from conventional. Aristophanes is known for his bawdy humour and wit, and the present company is exploiting them for all they're worth. 'It's one of the funniest and silliest plays I know, very up front and full of slapstick,' Laird says, during a rehearsal break. This element is likely to be highlighted by the costumes, which she says will be 'loud and cartoony'. But *Frogs*, generally accepted to be one of Aristophanes' best plays, also has its serious side, notably the famous debate in Hades between Aeschylus and Euripides about their contrasting methods of playwriting, with Dionysus holding the ring as umpire and Sophocles standing by to take on the winner.

Laird, who has directed productions of *The Clouds* and *Frogs* for her own touring company, has translated and adapted this version, using a very colloquial idiom. 'Some of the academic translations are very dull,' she says. 'I didn't want to chop the text about, I wanted to keep the spirit intact and make it work as Aristophanes wrote it.' She stresses that the play can stand up in its own right, and that, despite the political satire and contemporary references, audiences don't need to know anything about Greek culture in order to appreciate it. Since it is one of Aristophanes' later plays – it was first performed in 405 BC – the celebrated Greek chorus, in this case the frogs, plays a much less important role than it does in earlier plays. The bulk of the story concerns the eventful journey to the underworld made by Dionysus and his slave Xanthias.

Another unexpected element in the production is the music, which the company of five actors perform as an *a capella* quintet. Laird has written the music and lyrics herself ('I was brought up next to Ely Cathedral, so I love choral music'), using musical styles that range from do-wop to hip-hop. '*A capella* is very easy to manipulate with the actors, you don't have to wait for the orchestra to come in,' she says. 'It also solves the problem of how the chorus is handled – and of course it's cheap.' Given that this is a touring production, keeping costs down is important. But she also likes to put the accent on ensemble work, and believes this is helped by having the actors sing as well. 'I love the idea of all the actors doing everything,' she says, before getting back to the underworld.

Frogs opened in the Cottesloe in March 1996 and toured.

An epic challenge

Katie Mitchell ponders the problems of directing Ted Hughes' version of *The Oresteia*

I've always had a great love for Ted Hughes' work. When I was a child my father read *The Iron Man* to me and it stayed in my memory for years. As an adolescent I became obsessed with the poems in *Crow*. His version of *The Oresteia* is the most sustained and magnificent poem I've ever read. When Trevor Nunn asked me to direct it, I accepted it quicker than any other job offer in my whole life.

His new version of Aeschylus' trilogy was not a commission: he wrote it off his own bat. The nature of the writing is intensely intimate. He's flattened the epic meter, cut that away, and removed masses of references to Greek gods and other characters. He's gone for a very direct, simple, happening-in-the-kitchen style of writing that hits you between the eyeballs. There's not a line that flips off, that is flat or unconsidered, that isn't burning with deep passion for the material. If you just did it with four actors reading it on stage with microphones, it would still be an extraordinary experience.

The form is as important as in Shakespeare: you smash a line of Ted Hughes at your peril. The line divisions are very unexpected and they throw up unexpected meanings. He's very economical, he's trying to define each image so you don't lose anything, so the image never slips. It's almost like the actors are pressing the buttons on a slide projector to make sure the audience keep up with the images.

I suppose he was summing up his life in some sense. He's been true to Aeschylus, but because he's interested in certain ideas, he's taken them up and run with them a bit more. He's avoided the usual tendency to cut down the choruses, which make up over forty per cent of the plays. He's gone the other way and expanded them. And he's made the work more Christian, there's less of the Old Testament eye for an eye, and more mercy and forgiveness – although that's latent in the original.

He's also jacked up the murder of Iphigenia, which has only half the number of lines in the Greek. Certain images stand out, such as 'Pity is like a butterfly in a fist'. It's an exquisite poem about a father causing the death of his child and obviously very important to him. Someone said Hughes was trying on the clothes of the Greeks for size, to see if they fitted his own personal myth. So you ask yourself what myth or story he might be exorcising. But I think it would be pointless to compare what he is doing in *The Oresteia* with anything specific in his own life. I think it's much more complex than that.

It's been suggested that he has written up the horror in the plays. But I don't think he is getting off on violence, though he is very angry. I wonder whether it wasn't the Bosnian war that informed his writing. There's a predominance of images that tie in with that and the timing would be right. In the last play he changes 'civil strife' to 'civil war', so he's sharpened the meaning, and it becomes more anti-civil war.

He was such a pragmatist; he understood the mechanics of theatre, and everything he writes works. He wants to give a modern audience access to the plays and the ideas in them, and if anything is going to block that, he presses the eject button. It's such a profound sadness that he isn't alive, but it means that you look even more closely at the text to see what he was trying to communicate. The hard thing is finding production values that match his wonderful language and extraordinary images, making sure that you don't impose, straitjacket, reduce, or in any way diminish what he's written.

What makes *The Oresteia* unique, and so very different from other plays, is what Aeschylus is communicating, which is the agony of human experience, and the sophistication with which he communicates it, especially in the first two plays. It's also done on such a complex canvas, and his use of form is extraordinary. We're used to understanding drama through human situations, but not as debate or philosophical talk, or as storytelling in direct monologue fashion. So it's the form that is a real challenge for a director. It's like having a car you've never driven before, and you've got to dismantle it, put it back together again with the actors, and see if it will move.

We're starting with nothing. The production will not be a reconstruction of how they performed it in ancient Greece, with masks and togas, or of the Athenian society of the fifth century BC. Nor will it have a clearly contemporary setting like Bosnia or Northern Ireland, because that would patronise the experience of people who live in those countries, and reduce the meaning of the play. So we know what it's not going to be, but not what it is. That will have to come from the actors' collision with the material.

People are inevitably going to make comparisons with Peter Hall's 1981 production at the National, though I don't know if they will mean very much. That was a unique and extraordinary group of people communicating the play and Tony Harrison's text in a very specific way. I really respect what they did, but we are a very different group with a very different writer, working in a very different time. There have been so many changes since then, both positive and negative: Bosnia, South Africa and Mandela, Northern Ireland, the end of Thatcherism: all these have profoundly affected us morally and politically. The royal family is under threat, the Stephen Lawrence case has challenged our faith in legal systems, and we have not been in such a crisis over international justice since Nuremberg. These events have changed the meaning of the play, whatever form you do it in.

We're performing the trilogy in two parts, putting a knife through the second play, *The Libation Bearers*. You can justify doing this, because the titles of the plays were added fifty years after they were first produced in Athens: no one knows what they were called at the time. Normally in Greek theatre plays were named after the chorus or the protagonist, but in *The Oresteia* you have a mixture, which is inconsistent. So they're unreliable anyway.

The first play, *Agamemnon*, is the same length as the other two put together. But on its own it's an immoral play. Its message is: 'Go out and kill whoever you want and you'll be king and have a great time.' It's a celebration of the worst kind of violence. It's like saying, 'Hey Milosevic, go for it.' So you need to add part of the second play. There's also a problem with the resolution of the final play, *The Eumenides*, where Apollo says that Orestes should be let off for killing his mother, Clytemnestra, because mothers have nothing to do with their children's birth. It's a fantastically nasty, sexist argument, which is going to make most women in the audience go ballistic, and quite rightly.

Should you do *The Oresteia* with an all-male cast? I would only do that if the audience was also all-male. But you couldn't get that situation today. It would also be very hard to justify to the female acting profession, the fact that in this wonderful trilogy that has some of the best roles ever written for women, they should all be given to men. I think that would be indefensible.

The Oresteia opened in the Cottesloe in December 1999.

The readiness is all

Simon Russell Beale muses on his approach to playing Hamlet

It's a part I have always wanted to play. Along with Konstantin in *The Seagull* and Oswald in *Ghosts* it was in my private plan, the roles I wanted most to play. The problem was, I was an unlikely casting for them all, being short and stocky, and not a romantic actor. But I managed to do Konstantin and Oswald, and loved playing them.

Hamlet was talked about while I was at the Royal Shakespeare Company, and I got very close to playing him at the Donmar. More recently I was going to do it at the National with Sam Mendes, but his career became complicated with

American Beauty. Last year, while we were rehearsing *Money* at the National, John Caird asked me to do it with him. I'm thirty-nine, so I thought, I've got to do it now. Even then I didn't believe it would happen until the first day of rehearsal.

Normally I don't do any preparation before rehearsals begin – I'm not very good at working by myself. But this time I did. As there are so many words, I thought I'd better start learning the part, although in the cut version it probably isn't as long as Iago, which I played recently at the National. For two months before we started rehearsing John and I met once a week, and read an act together. That was very valuable: I love John's intellectual excitement. He's also one of the most collaborative directors I know, incredibly open and generous to other people's ideas, which is a great strength.

Thinking of all the other actors who have played Hamlet is a bit of a nightmare. Fortunately I haven't seen that many, which is a good thing – not for my soul, perhaps, but certainly for playing it. In fact, when you start rehearsing it's not really a problem, because of the nature of the part. Hamlet is really what you want to make of him. It's a part that gives you an extraordinary sense of using yourself. Iago is like a mosaic, it's little bits of naturalistic behaviour that you build up to make a more composite picture of evil. With Hamlet it's more of a question of looking into yourself, which in a way makes it more difficult. He's so much more of a conduit than Iago or Richard III, whom I've also played. There's an everyman quality about him, something essentially simple, which I think is probably best served by not trying to be too clever. So I don't really have any game plan, because I don't think the part demands it.

I was worried about the madness, whether I would have to do something extraordinary like standing on my head. But I'm not very good at tricks or inventing bits of business; I'm not the type. So I suspect in the end it's going to be quite a simple Hamlet. I know I'd like him to be funny, and I flatter myself that the wit and the wryness and the self-deprecation will be all right. The difficult part will be the huge waves of emotional power. You could spend so much time sobbing and I don't want to do that. I don't want to force emotion, I need to get there slowly, to get the emotional arc right, and not find too many moments of crisis.

Grief plays a large part in Hamlet's condition and that's something I'm experiencing now, for the first time in my life. A few weeks ago my mother died. She was an extraordinary woman, and my relationship with her was a very close and loving one. Yet at this moment my overriding emotion is one of frustration, because I seem incapable of feeling enough. That may be appropriate for the part, but it's a bitter preparation for playing it – although I know Ralph Fiennes went through the same misery of a mother's early death before *he* played Hamlet, so I'm not alone.

As a girl, my mother used to switch off the light in her bedroom and listen to Olivier performing some of Hamlet's great soliloquies. For me it's a privilege to be able, with her, to explore the greatest meditations on grief and death ever written. My performance will be a kind of tribute to her.

Hamlet opened in the Lyttelton in September 2000.

Pushing back the boundaries

David Harewood argues that Othello is a role that belongs to black actors

He is the National's first black Othello but not, he sincerely hopes, the last. Talking during rehearsals for Sam Mendes' current production of Shakespeare's great tragedy, David Harewood makes clear straight away what his views are on the notorious 'blacking-up' issue.

'In the last twenty years several top white actors have played Othello with boot polish on,' he says. 'I find it quite strange that they were still doing that until about five years ago. But now there are plenty of fine black actors who could play the part, so we don't need to do it any more.' He has seen the film of Laurence Olivier's controversial 1964 'negro' performance at the National, which he reluctantly admits to admiring for its display of technical skills. 'But here was this white man with a blackamoor's face' – and he breaks off to do a pastiche version of Olivier's 'black' voice and eye-rolling technique.

David Harewood, now thirty-one, is no stranger to Shakespeare: after the National Youth Theatre's *As You Like It* he played Romeo for Temba and Edmund in *King Lear* for Talawa, and has recently been Antony to Vanessa Redgrave's Cleopatra. He's also played the Moor before, some five years ago at the Swan in Worcester. 'Then it was simply a case of learning the lines and getting on the stage,' he recalls. 'I've done a lot of theatre outside the big companies, but this is the first time since drama school that anyone has really picked me up on anything like verse, diction and phrasing. It's very exciting, because you think, this is not just a job, it's a craft.'

He's done plenty of background reading for the part, especially on the subject of the spread of Western Islam. He's opted to create an Othello with a North African accent who comes from a well-to-do Muslim dynasty, seeing him as a scholar as much as a soldier, a learned and intelligent man who is nevertheless naïve when it comes to dealing with ordinary human affairs. 'He's a man who's travelled a lot, who's had to adapt, who's been taken into and then released from slavery,' he explains. 'He would have had to excel in a particular way to get where he was in the Venetian army, and one of the many challenges he had was learning a foreign language.'

His reading has also led him to reflect on the position of black people in Elizabethan England, and to a conviction that by creating a noble, if flawed, Moor, Shakespeare was aiming to change his contemporaries' perceptions of them as 'all liars and good-for-nothings'. 'I believe Shakespeare was trying to make people realise that there was more to black people than they thought,' he suggests. 'He was saying, "Hang on, who are these people walking around our streets, carrying bags and being treated very badly? They come from their own civilisations, their own kingdoms, and yet over here they're nothing."'

Meanwhile there are today's attitudes. He agrees integrated

casting has become more accepted recently – but not every-where. He's just been playing Antony in a predominantly black *Julius Caesar* in Houston, Texas, where there were rumblings of discontent in the audience. 'It's still contentious, so we have to keep pushing at the boundaries,' he says. He'd like to play a black Iago, but believes that kind of experiment is some way off. Meanwhile he hopes his Othello might lead to some shift in the composition of the National's audience. 'I came to several shows here last year and most of the time I was the only black person in the audience. People looked at me as if to say, "What are you doing here?"'

Othello opened in the Cottesloe in September 1997.

Fascinating and glamorous

Sean Mathias relishes the prospect of directing *Antony and Cleopatra*

In the past certain critics and academics have refused to include *Antony and Cleopatra* among Shakespeare's tragedies, on the grounds that its two deeply flawed characters neither deserve nor get our sympathy. To Sean Mathias, who is about to direct the play for the National, this is complete nonsense.

'I don't see how one can fail to empathise with them, they're so completely fascinating and glamorous, and their flaws are so attractive,' he says. 'I find their dilemma very moving and I think it's one that speaks to a modern audience. Besides, I've always enjoyed directing actors playing people who are considered monsters, trying to deconstruct them and find a human side.'

Talking before rehearsals start, he reveals that this is his first attempt at directing Shakespeare. 'Although I admire his work, I had no real interest until recently,' he admits. 'You either get great productions or terrible ones; so few are really inspiring.' Into the inspirational category he puts Giorgio Strehler's

The Tempest, Trevor Nunn's Stratford *Macbeth*, and Mark Rylance's interpretation of Hamlet.

Although he claims he's excited to be entering virgin territory as a director, he could hardly have chosen a more challenging piece with which to make his Shakespearean debut. With its forty scenes and thirty speaking parts, and a potential running time of four hours if no cuts are made, *Antony and Cleopatra* presents considerable logistical problems, never mind the artistic ones. But Mathias seems unfazed by the prospect, citing his determination to develop a strong ensemble sense in his company. 'I can't make the production alone,' he says. 'I want the actors playing messengers and other small roles to be integral to the play, not marginalised and merely servants of the two main characters. A lot of the physicality will come from them.'

As with other productions he's done, he intends to spend the first two weeks or so of rehearsal doing a range of exercises with the actors – for example, getting them to play each other's roles – to help them build up the desired ensemble spirit. The process, he believes, should be a journey of discovery for him as much as for them: 'I do a play to find out what it's about, I don't come knowing what it's about and then do it.'

There have, of course, been some celebrated performances and productions of the play over the years. One of the more controversial was the pale-skinned, red-haired Cleopatra at Stratford of Peggy Ashcroft, who emphasised the character's guile and chameleon-like qualities rather than her voluptuousness. Janet Suzman, also playing at Stratford, was acclaimed for capturing Cleopatra's lethal combination of sexuality and intellect. Glenda Jackson has also played Cleopatra there – as indeed has Helen Mirren, opposite Michael Gambon at the Other Place and the Pit in 1982.

But the production that still comes most vividly to mind for many people is Peter Hall's at the National in 1987, with Judi Dench and Anthony Hopkins in the lead roles. Hall was widely praised for his control of the narrative and for allowing the text to exert its magic. Dench's spitfire Cleopatra dazzled the critics, with its speed, power and sheer range of emotion.

Hopkins' performance was admired by some, but the actor himself, like others before him, disliked the role: 'Antony is a dreadful part – you just lumber around the stage in a bad temper and then die,' he said later.

Although he saw the Hall production, Sean Mathias doesn't feel its shadow across his shoulder. 'I have no strong recollection of it,' he admits. 'I don't consider having seen that or other productions of the play a handicap, because they tend to become fragmented in my memory. Anyway, you just have to aim to make your own production special, to make it for now.' He's already relishing the idea of working with such an established and versatile actress as Helen Mirren. 'The poignancy of the play is that Antony and Cleopatra are older people who have done something remarkable with their lives, yet we see them sparring and playing childish games with each other. You can still see the girl in Helen: her youth has accompanied her into middle age, and that doesn't happen with everyone.'

He saw and admired her Cleopatra at Stratford and, though he's not worked with her before, thinks her qualities will fit the role superbly. 'She has tremendous glamour and charisma, while still seeming to be an ordinary woman,' he says. 'She seems to combine street cred with that glamour, which makes her a very modern actress. She is also a sensualist and that's important. Although it's a play about power as well as love, it's not a public play, it's a very intimate one.'

A voyage of rediscovery

Helen Mirren looks forward to her third Cleopatra

Cleopatra is not a difficult part to play in terms of its language, which is very beautiful and easy to grasp. The only difficulty is that you're playing the legend. Everyone has their own ideas about her, so you can never hope to fulfil their expectations.

Playing Lady Macbeth or Ophelia is more difficult than

playing Cleopatra. They come on, they disappear for several scenes, and come back mad. So then you have to twist the text into all kinds of pretzel shapes in order to find the character. With Cleopatra, she's just a person, a very rounded human being. Her complexity makes it easier to find the logic of the part.

This will be my third Cleopatra. At eighteen I played it for the National Youth Theatre. I loved it. At that age you don't think, how will I cope with this part? You just jump in. You're very emotional, self-involved, romantic and imaginative, which makes the imaginative leap you need to make so much easier.

My second Cleopatra was in Adrian Noble's production at the Other Place in Stratford in 1982, with Michael Gambon playing Antony. Adrian wanted to take a fresh look at the play and do it as a chamber piece, so we did it on a bare, naked stage. He left me pretty free to play the part as I wanted. But it helped enormously to have played it before – especially since I found that I still remembered the lines.

I saw Glenda Jackson's performance at Stratford, but missed Judi Dench's at the National. But if I had seen it I don't think it would have inhibited my playing of the part. If I'd never done it before it might have been difficult, but I know the play so well now. I don't usually do any research for a part and I didn't before with Cleopatra. But this time I'm curious, so I'm going to do some good old-fashioned historical research, and try to learn as much as possible about the real person outside the play.

My hunger to play Cleopatra again is born partly of desperation, because I know I'm probably never going to do it again. It's my last chance to get it even half right. The wonder and excitement but also the fear of these big roles is that you never know what's going to happen. So it's going to be a real voyage of discovery for me.

Antony and Cleopatra opened in the Olivier in October 1998.

Modern magic

Nicholas Hytner reflects on the powerful appeal of *The Winter's Tale*

What attracts me to the play as a director is the fact that it deals with very basic questions. I've come to believe more and more that Shakespeare's plays aren't necessarily difficult or complicated, but deep-probing and resonant expressions of basic, simple perceptions and feelings about life.

Time passes in *The Winter's Tale* and shatters the illusions of those who grow older. Nobody can be 'boy eternal'. Husbands turn on their wives, fathers turn on their children, the grave beckons. But in these last plays Shakespeare balances the savagery of the natural cycle with the joy of rebirth. Simultaneously you get the tragic, subjective view of the human predicament and the eternal optimism of youth. There's always a new generation, idealistic and hopeful; there's enough joy to revitalise even those who have ruined their own lives if they'll open themselves up to it.

It can, of course, seem like two separate plays, with a vivid and dramatic split between the intense, disturbing psychodrama of the first half and the energy, anarchy and joy of the second. But that doesn't worry me: I think they should be as different as possible. I don't feel you should homogenise something that Shakespeare has taken enormous trouble to differentiate. And in the end it becomes an organic whole.

I've decided to use a contemporary setting. Nowadays I think you have to have a very good reason *not* to do that. The story is in fact very modern: here are wealthy, powerful people in early middle age doing what they've always done, staying in each other's homes, flirting with each other's wives – and then, bang. After all, there's nothing remote about a man who suddenly feels his wife is in love with his best friend, or a man furious about the company his son is keeping and the girl he wants to spend his life with, or a group of kids getting together to sing and dance. The challenge will be to make the play magical without falling back on nostalgia, without patronising the past by giving it a golden glow, but by seeking what is eternally mythic in the lives we lead now.

The climactic scene, when Hermione comes back to life, is a special challenge, but it always seems to work in the theatre. What is wonderful about it is how Shakespeare obsessively advertises the fact that what he's about to show you is incredible: 'so like an old tale', 'Like an old tale still', 'That she is living, were it but told you, should be hooted at like an old tale'. He's saying: this is the theatre, it's all art, it's not true; but I've written thirty-five plays already, and I'm so in charge of my art that I can rub your face in its artifice and you'll still believe it. I can make you believe the dead can come back to life. My art is truer than life.

Making Leontes' jealousy credible is more of a problem in the study than on the stage. We're familiar with breakdowns, with midlife crises: I look around and see people for no good reason walking out of good relationships, turning on their partners, seized with rage and self-loathing. For an actor the switch from bland contentment to pathological destructiveness is sudden, but I think psychologically acute. Jealousy is irrational, requires no motivation, and is so often a symptom of something else. There's a very strong suggestion in the first scene that Leontes has failed to grow up, and that's something I want to explore in rehearsal.

Apart from being able to get under the skin and inside the skull of a character, Alex Jennings, who plays Leontes, is also one of only a handful of actors who can draw in the people farthest away from him in a space like the Olivier. He has skills that are rapidly becoming defunct: actors today don't have a career like his, which involved going through all the reps and not being thrust into the main theatres until he was fully equipped to play in them.

I love the Olivier Theatre, it's an exciting and generous space to work in. I dislike the growing tendency to stage Shakespeare in small spaces. Theatrical fashion is now created by a tiny number of people who've become seduced by the faintly narcissistic pleasures of seeing large plays in small rooms in the company of each other. It's like Versailles: court theatres for the metropolitan elite. It's fine to be among the elect, but the large, public element of Shakespeare's plays disappears. And because they're a hundred times easier to act in a small space, so actors and directors and designers are gradually losing their skill. That distresses me.

The Winter's Tale opened in the Olivier in May 2001.

Father–son relationships

Matthew Macfadyen looks forward to playing Prince Hal in the two parts of *Henry IV*

Despite his recent successes in film and television, Matthew Macfadyen's heart clearly belongs to the theatre. 'It's five years now since I've done a play and I feel so happy to be back,' he says. 'Theatre is what I started off doing, it's live and I love it. Of course there is repetition and often tedium, but when it works well, it's really worth it.'

We're talking in the early days of rehearsals for the two parts of *Henry IV*, the opening production in the third Travelex £10 season in the Olivier, in which director Nicholas Hytner has cast him as Prince Hal. It's only his second appearance at the National; his first, back in 1999, was as Mr Brougham in Nick Stafford's *Battle Royal*. Since then there's been an impressive variety of leading roles in major television dramas, including Stephen Poliakoff's *Perfect Strangers*, the adaptation of Trollope's *The Way We Live Now* and most recently *Spooks*. His film career also looks set to take wing: he's soon to be seen as Mr Darcy in *Pride and Prejudice*, the first actor to play the part on the big screen since Laurence Olivier in 1940.

Theatre seems to have been in the family genes: his grandfather directed plays as an amateur, his mother trained as an actress and drama teacher. At Oakham School in Leicestershire he soon got hooked on acting. 'The theatre studies department was fantastic. I did about eighteen plays: we toured to Edinburgh, we even went once to Texas. It was probably to the detriment of my GCSEs, but it was brilliant.' While at school he went through the motions of applying to university, while secretly applying to drama schools. He went straight to RADA at seventeen. 'I think it was the right decision. If I'd gone to university I would just have done a few plays, drunk beer and got a terrible degree.' From RADA he joined Declan Donnellan's company Cheek by Jowl, and spent his first three years doing nothing but theatre.

Tall, sporting a light beard ('It's not for the part, it's just laziness') and engagingly modest, he's fascinated by the role of Prince Hal, but admits he's still feeling his way into the part. 'Hal doesn't want to grow up, but he has this terrible responsibility hanging over his head. His father–son relationships, with both the king and Falstaff, are very simple, but also very complicated. In these early days I'm still swimming about a bit. A lot of the play feels very dense – but then Nick Hytner helps you suddenly to unlock it and it just flies.'

He's no newcomer to Shakespeare, having played Demetrius in Adrian Noble's RSC production of *A Midsummer Night's Dream*, and more recently Benedick in the Cheek by Jowl version of *Much Ado About Nothing*. But Prince Hal is a challenge of a different order. 'Benedick is mostly prose and Demetrius more slapstick than poetry. Hal, on the other hand, has great swathes of verse and that's quite daunting. I swing between being utterly thrilled and just terrified.'

He speaks very positively of the two parts of *Henry IV*, which are often underrated in the Shakespeare canon. 'They're really good plays, much better than I thought they were, and they stand alone from each other. One of the misconceptions is that Part 2 is a sequel, but actually they're dramatically different in tone. Part 1 is full of *joie de vivre*, whereas Part 2, when Hal becomes Henry V and banishes Falstaff and all his frippery, is very sad.'

Falstaff is played by Michael Gambon, something of a boyhood hero for Macfadyen; they worked together on *Perfect Strangers*. 'It's glorious watching him and rehearsing with him. He's very funny and very generous, and a fascinating mixture:

he has elements of the clown but also of the statesman; it's all in there. I think he'll be a wonderful Falstaff.'

Henry IV Parts 1 and 2 opened in the Olivier in April 2005.

He who plays the king

After his acclaimed Hamlet, Adrian Lester takes on the title role in *Henry V*

'I always remember myself as a schoolkid, watching a play at Stratford, wanting to understand it, but being so bored by the terrible Shakespeare delivery. So I want to be sure I communicate the meaning of this play to those who haven't been to university, who haven't read all the books and know every line.'

Calm, sensitive and intelligent, yet full of determination and latent fire, Adrian Lester seems perfectly cast for the title role in *Henry V*. Not even the ghosts of Henrys past, or the surviving interpretations on film by Laurence Olivier and Kenneth Branagh, seem to intimidate him, as he prepares to go into battle next month in Nicholas Hytner's production. 'That tradition, the many great actors who have played Henry, may make it seem like a daunting task,' he says. 'But I'm more concerned about the huge amount there is to do with the part, and the energy I'll need throughout to get over its full meaning.'

His school in Birmingham gave little time or space to the arts, so he joined a cathedral choir and later a youth theatre based at the Midlands Arts Centre, where he attended ballet, contemporary dance and martial arts classes. 'All my interests were taking place out of school, and the youth theatre was my second home,' he recalls. 'It was a battle between homework and rehearsals – and I'm afraid rehearsals won.'

At RADA he did plenty of work on Shakespeare, but never acted in a full-length production. Since then, however, he's been well immersed in the plays, with *As You Like It* (twice) and *A Midsummer Night's Dream* already under his belt, not to mention the film of *Love's Labour's Lost*, where his dance lessons clearly paid off. He's also shown an impressive versatility, from his many roles on film, through *Six Degrees of Separation*, to his engaging performance in Sondheim's musical, *Company*. But it was his dark, very modern Hamlet, directed by Peter Brook for a world tour a couple of years ago, that really set audiences and critics alight.

'A week before rehearsals began I sat down with Peter in his room in Paris, and we went through the big speeches very quietly and slowly,' he recalls. 'I was struck by the fact that Hamlet was a very witty man, in love with acting and performance, but someone who was struggling not to lose his mind, as he considered life and found it so painful and full of betrayal and wrongdoing. Peter gave me the courage to be introspective: by the end I felt I had gone to places within myself that I hadn't been to before.' He also discussed the role with Kenneth Branagh, asking him if there was anything he knew after playing Hamlet that he wished he'd known before. 'He talked about how easy it was to get lost in the books, to find yourself playing the explanations rather than getting in touch with your own response to the role.'

Before receiving the call to arms from Nicholas Hytner, Lester had already seen Olivier's stirring 1944 film which, through judicious cuts to the text, presented an essentially heroic Henry for wartime audiences. Then he saw Branagh's version: 'I thought it was fantastic. It wasn't pretty or beautifully described, which would have had me switching off. It was full of mud and sweat and tears, he really gave it a life. When it's done like that it bypasses your intellect and hits you in the gut.'

He's very conscious of this being the National's first main-stage production (there was an NT Education touring workshop production in 1994), and that he'll be playing in a theatre with a name and history that has a particular resonance for 'he who plays the king'. But his interpretation seems likely to differ significantly from Olivier's patriotic warrior-king. 'He's a complex character, he's really a mirror, so that whatever anyone wants to see in him, they see,' he says. 'It may be the pious and godly king, or the young diplomat skilled at playing different parties off against each other, or the wooer of Katharine, apparently completely lovesick. He's all things to all people, he's very pliable, and I want to play all those facets, not just one of them. It's like a polka-dot painting – if you look too closely you'll see just one colour, but if you step back you'll see the whole character in your head.'

Henry V opened in the Olivier in May 2003.

Answering the right questions

Simon McBurney on the key to staging
Measure for Measure

When the National's director Nicholas Hytner invited Simon McBurney and Complicite to stage a Shakespeare play, he suggested *A Midsummer Night's Dream* to them. But the director of the celebrated innovative ensemble declined the offer. 'I said I had no desire to create Complicite fairies,' he recalls. 'I also felt the play had already been done marvellously by so many other people.'

So they settled on *Measure for Measure*, a play he had always loved and thought he knew well. 'Then I read it again and wondered what I'd let myself in for. It's a great work, but a very difficult one, full of complicated imagery. It's also very tricky in plot terms, and much of the action takes place off stage. I realised I didn't understand it – and that was still the case on the first day of rehearsal.'

Talking before the opening of the revival of his much-praised production, McBurney stresses that he likes to start rehearsals without pre-planning. 'A lot of directors come in with a concept, but I'm essentially an actor, so I explore the play from the inside out. I also like to work with the designer in rehearsal, rather than have it all worked out beforehand.

This also gives me a chance to work in tandem with the other actors.'

His normal practice with Complicite productions is to tell the story to friends or relatives before starting rehearsals. 'When I make a piece of theatre it's important to know that people understand the shape, the rhythm and the architecture,' he says. 'Doing this gives me a strong sense of what particularly interests people. I tell the story in different forms and it's fascinating to see what arrests them.' With *Measure for Measure* he found his teenage niece very gripped by the story: 'She understood the play's issues of sex and power, of authority and punishment.'

Since the founding of Complicite the company has worked on five Shakespeare plays and produced two of them, the first being *The Winter's Tale* in 1992. McBurney likens working on Shakespeare to learning a different dialect. 'It's always a long process, because the language is not quite our own. For *Measure for Measure* I delayed any decisions about the set and staging, so that the principal focus could be on the language.' He found what is generally seen as one of Shakespeare's more problematic plays a very curious one, full of anomalies: 'The more you investigate it, the more it's clear that other writers as well as Shakespeare are involved. It's full of clunky stage business, and many bits of it felt as if they were in the wrong place. But once we cut certain parts or lines it seemed to make sense.'

For the first three weeks of the eight-week rehearsal period the actors just spoke the text over and over again, without any pause and without doing any acting. This, McBurney says, helped them to understand its poetry and rhythm. 'Because most of it is poetry, the meaning is not always explicit, and is often implied. There's a musical meaning, a percussive use of words, which you can only get when you speak them.'

He's in no doubt that this apparently profligate use of precious rehearsal time paid off. 'I see so many Shakespeare productions where I don't know where I am, or what the characters are doing. The answers to these two questions deliver everything. So in rehearsal we spent an enormous amount of time establishing what they were and what Shakespeare intended. Only then could we decide how to make all this explicit to an audience and how to make clear where a character is going emotionally.'

Playing Angelo and Isabella

Paul Rhys and Naomi Frederick explore the key characters in *Measure for Measure*

Paul Rhys on Angelo

I was asked to play Angelo many years ago by the Royal Shakespeare Company, but I didn't understand him at all, so I said no. I didn't like him, I found him very cold and dark. But I accepted the National's offer because I wanted to challenge myself – and also because if any director can unearth the extraordinary architecture of *Measure for Measure* it's Simon McBurney.

It's still a relatively unknown play: not that long ago it had the reputation for emptying theatres. But it's a work that's much more understandable to us now, perhaps because we are psychologically more introspective. It has a lot of themes, sex and religion being the dominant ones, and very complex meanings, rhythms and verse. I see parallels all over the place with *Macbeth*.

Having played Hamlet certainly helps me with Angelo, as playing Shakespeare on any level would. I haven't seen any previous productions, but I think that's an advantage. Anyway there's no definitive performance of Angelo, so he comes quite uncluttered by the past; it's a part you have to filter totally through your own understanding. Similarly, the play has no famous incidents or images, such as the blinding of Gloucester or Hamlet talking to Yorick's skull or the Forest of Arden, where the audience come wondering how these moments are going to be handled.

Within the world of the play there's hardly a character who doesn't have a view of Angelo. His name is on virtually every page of the text; on one page it comes up ten times. It's a world that's slightly obsessed with him and yet he's not in the play for quite a lot of the time. It's very peculiar. I've found him a fascinating character psychologically. He's understandable to us now, and perhaps in Shakespeare's day he was too, but to the Victorians he wasn't. He's a deeply repressed man, but he's made whole by his experience: through adversity he achieves unity.

Academics often refer to him as the villain, but this seems to me a gross distortion. Within his own terms he has enormous honour and consistency, he absolutely obeys what he sees to be the subjugation of the personal to the law, even when he realises he has done wrong. I don't believe his violent reaction to seeing Isabella is simply lust. He's struck by her virtue, by the purity of her. In many ways he sees her as a female version of himself. People often talk about finding their other half, and Angelo and Isabella certainly talk each other's language. Within seconds they're finishing each other's sentences; it's an extraordinary mirror.

Angelo is a continuation of Oedipus, who was perhaps the first character in the theatre to examine himself emotionally. All the soliloquies in *Measure for Measure* are his, and even if he can also be seen as the Angel, or the Fall, he's clearly very human. We're all him really, so this internal struggle makes him sympathetic to us. His honest self-examination, of a kind we're more used to now, makes him seem very modern.

Naomi Frederick on Isabella

I saw Claire Skinner as Isabella at the Young Vic when I was sixteen, and I was blown away. It was one of the productions that made me desperately want to work in the theatre, and Isabella is a part that's stayed in my mind ever since.

When I studied the play at school, I thought that at some deep level Isabella was frightened of sex, that jumping into bed with a man was something she couldn't confront. But when I looked for the fear this time I couldn't find it, and I don't think it's there. She's just very resolute and strong: she's made this decision to join a nunnery with all its restraint and rules, and she's not about to break them.

I think the audience needs to be on her side, so they don't see her decision as harsh and unfair. There would certainly be no question of a nun sleeping with someone in order to save her brother's life. But then she hasn't become a nun yet, and I question what she's doing in the first place, signing on at this nunnery. It's certainly not clear from the text. The first time we see her she's a novice, she's literally just arrived. She's extremely bright and clear thinking, but naïve almost because of the clarity of her thought, because she doesn't see outside her own intentions.

Both she and Claudio have sharp intellects. He persuades her to plead with Angelo because he knows she's up to it. Later he tries to get the better of her by saying, 'Have you thought that if I die, this is what it will be like to be dead?' She's taken in, but when he suggests that sleeping with Angelo to save his life won't be considered a sin, she realises he's just trying to win her over, and she's not having any of that. So her cleverness and clarity are her greatest strengths, and I'm sure that's where Shakespeare started from.

There's a danger for the actress playing Isabella: you can very easily hit top gear very quickly and never come down. The poor audience would then be sitting there having this desperate woman shouting at them all evening. That would be terrible and unwatchable. But the way Simon McBurney is directing us has, I hope, given me the scope to find a whole range of ways of playing the lines and avoiding that trap.

Measure for Measure opened in the Olivier in May 2004, and was revived in the Lyttelton in March 2006.

ENGLISH AND IRISH CLASSICS

Virtue under siege

Matthew Warchus shares his ideas about Ben Jonson and *Volpone*

Ben Jonson's classic comedy is essentially a play about greed, about the extraordinary lengths people will go to in their pursuit of wealth. For director Matthew Warchus that's a theme that resonates very clearly in our own times. 'Of course greed was more pervasive in the Thatcherite 1980s, it was more part of the political culture,' he says. 'But today there are still events that intrigue and horrify us, such as the national lottery. I'm sure many artists will soon be responding to that.'

Making his debut at the National, and following in the footsteps of Tyrone Guthrie and Peter Hall in tackling *Volpone*, Warchus already has considerable experience of Jonson's work: his first production after university was *Sejanus, His Fall* and he's recently directed *The Devil is an Ass* for the Royal Shakespeare Company at the Swan in Stratford. So what's the special attraction of this master of language, rated only second to Shakespeare in his time?

'I'm interested in his directness and bluntness, the way he channels his anger through humour and satire,' he says. 'He lived in a very bleak society, where there were few moments of joy or colour. He spent a lot of time considering the ugliness of human nature, lifting up a stone and finding some dreadful creatures underneath.' Surprisingly, he doesn't see Jonson as an out-and-out pessimist. 'Deep down I think he was truly optimistic. He had these great slumps of cynicism, but they were followed by bursts of creative optimism,' he says. 'After all, the very fact of putting his ideas into plays shows a kind of optimism, believing that people might be affected by them.'

In *Volpone*, he suggests, Jonson cleverly gets the best of both worlds. 'He encourages you to enjoy the vices of his characters, but then when he weaves the story you start to pull away. Something that seems funny at first becomes terribly bad when you look more closely.' Yet despite Jonson's clear moral purpose in having Mosca and Volpone self-destruct, the devil does seem to have all the best lines: the only two virtuous characters are but sketchily drawn and play little part in the two villains' downfall. Warchus doesn't necessarily see this as a failing. 'The fact that these characters are weak is a reflection of reality,' he argues. 'In the perpetual war between vice and virtue, it's virtue that is always under siege, always in the minority.'

But Jonson's appeal, he argues, lies not just in his clear-eyed view of human foibles. 'He's also a brilliant craftsman, who writes complex stories that are completely thought through. He doesn't leave all kinds of loose ends, as Shakespeare so often does.' The wealth of classical and contemporary allusions, however, presents a problem, which he's solved by cutting 800 of the play's 3,000 lines. 'Jonson interacted a lot with his own time, but because of that some of his satire dates.'

There have, however, been no problems over casting. Matthew Warchus believes he's found the ideal Volpone and Mosca in Michael Gambon and Simon Russell Beale. 'Michael is very rascally, he's someone with an incredible sense of humour who can never stop playing. And Simon has this mercurial quality, an amazing ability to change his shape and personality. They fit the parts perfectly.'

Volpone opened in the Olivier in July 1995.

A play for today

Nicholas Hytner believes Etherege's comedy
The Man of Mode is totally up to date

'It's a wonderful play about young people with a terrific fascination with money, sex and fashion. Does that sound familiar?' *The Man of Mode* may belong to the seventeenth century, but Nicholas Hytner, the director of the National's current production, feels it could have been written yesterday. Those three obsessions that characterised the glittering society of the Restoration period are, he suggests, much in evidence in twenty-first-century Britain.

Written in 1676, the play is considered George Etherege's masterpiece. It bursts with sexual intrigue with no holds barred, in a world preoccupied with wit, scandal and the latest fashion, where outward appearances belie the basic desires and ambitions of its characters. Its hero, Dorimant, allegedly based on the notorious libertine Lord Rochester, is shameless in pursuit of his next mistress, but eventually meets his match in the independent and resourceful Harriet.

The play also features a glorious comic creation in the shape of that monument to affectation, Sir Fopling Flutter. Hytner has no difficulty in identifying his modern equivalents. 'There are so many people on the fringes of fashion, with a gap between who they are and who they think they are,' he says. 'David Beckham is a prime example. Of course, he has a job and is skilled at it, but outside that he has an obsession with the glittering surface of things.'

There have been only two Restoration comedies at the National in the last twelve years: *The Relapse* by John Vanbrugh, directed by Trevor Nunn in 2001, and Phyllida Lloyd's production of Congreve's *The Way of the World* in 1995. 'I love these plays and I thought it was high time we did another one,' Hytner explains.

The Man of Mode is an insider's play: Etherege was himself part of the clique of wits gathered around Charles II whose manners and behaviour he satirises. A poet and musician as well as a playwright, he behaved in private like one of his own stage gallants, drinking and revelling and pursuing actresses. This perhaps partly explains the genial, detached nature of the satire. 'There's no moral point of view, it's not a play that is interested in judgements,' Hytner argues. 'Etherege neither approves nor disapproves of his characters' conduct. Unlike Ben Jonson, who observed behaviour on the dungheap from a million miles away, he is writing from within that world. So there's a relish for it, but also a humane awareness of the pain that people go through.'

To point up the play's absolute modernity he's set it in modern dress. 'I do think an audience will always view a play written three or four hundred years ago through the filter of the present. They can never be totally immersed in the original period; they're always aware of making connections with today's world. And whether a production is played in the original period, or in the present, that tension between the two worlds is always exciting.'

As a director he likes to work on plays that have authenticity and energy, qualities he feels Etherege's hard-hitting, realistic comedy has in abundance. 'It also has great wit and eloquence: the characters speak well, which is one reason why it's so alive. And it shows brilliantly how little we have travelled since that time.'

The Man of Mode opened in the Olivier in January 2007.

The heart of Congreve

Phyllida Lloyd takes issue with the idea of *The Way of the World* as a Restoration comedy

'*The Way of the World* is actually a very end-of-century play that looks forward in an astonishing way to Ibsen and Chekhov.' Phyllida Lloyd, the director of the National's production of Congreve's masterpiece, has wanted to tackle the play for a long time. Now she's done so, she finds herself at variance with the received wisdom about its nature.

'I think it's wrongly dubbed a Restoration comedy, although it's got on to school syllabuses as such,' she says. 'Although it was first performed in 1700, it tends to get lumped in with the Restoration comedies, as other late-seventeenth-century plays do. Yet it's not even James, it's William and Mary.'

But it's not just the play's historical period that she questions. 'It's turned out to be as bleak as it is funny,' she says. 'Like, for example, *The Importance of Being Earnest*, it's a very clever play. But in terms of heart there's no comparison between the two. Congreve's play not only has greater complexity than Wilde's, it also expresses a sense of grief and loss.'

While she agrees that much of the play resonates with the Restoration period, she feels there is plenty that does not. 'There's its ambiguity, the blurring of the characters' morality, so that you can't just identify them as good or bad. I think in their mixture of agony and acceptance they're very Chekhovian.' In Restoration comedies, she argues, perhaps two-thirds of the characters are complex enough to allow the actors scope to explore their inner life, while the rest are just on the surface. In *The Way of the World*, however, every single character can stand that kind of scrutiny.

She cites the ageing Lady Wishfort as an example. 'She's not just an idiotic character, she shows how to have expectations of love or of being desired in old age is ridiculous – and that's both hilarious and ghastly. She provides a deeply moving and affecting picture of the idiocy and agony of old age.'

So how helpful is Congreve's own distinction between true wits and false wits? 'The distinction is there, but I don't want to splinter the characters into the wise and the silly,' she says. 'A true wit has judgement; but if you don't have that, it doesn't mean you don't have an inner life.'

Congreve has been described as a master of feminine psychology. Unusually for the period, *The Way of the World* has four very substantial female parts, of which Millamant is both the most scintillating and the most challenging. 'She's flighty, flirty, coquettish, coy, quick in thought, intelligent – a true wit,' Lloyd observes. 'But she's not incapable of feeling pain. Her single life is free but vapid, and you see how desperate she is. Yet she has this enormous fear of losing her independence, which means she makes huge conditions for her life with Mirabell.'

From her director's standpoint she believes Fiona Shaw makes an ideal Millamant. 'I can't think of anybody in whom the gap between thought and word is less discernible,' she says. 'You can't spot the join. Her mercurial mind and speed of thought invariably match Congreve's quickness of imagination.'

The Way of the World opened in the Lyttelton in October 1995.

Low character and dubious taste

Max Stafford-Clark is rehearsing Oliver Goldsmith's classic *She Stoops to Conquer*

It's not a typical rehearsal. The props and set have just been sent on to Oxford, where *She Stoops to Conquer* opens next week. The rehearsal room in the National is almost bare, so the actors have to make do with the odd chair and a well-used sofa.

By now the broad shape of the production has been settled. This morning director Max Stafford-Clark is working on the fine detail, suggesting an alternative motive here, rethinking a piece of business there. He's hot on the text, insisting the actors speak Goldsmith's exact words. He encourages the country characters – Tony Lumpkin, the Hardcastles – to go for their Midlands accents with greater relish.

'*She Stoops to Conquer* is a wonderful play, a sure-fire comedy,' he says, during a break in the rehearsal. 'You never really know a play until you direct it, but my admiration for Goldsmith has gone up and up. It's ironic that what we now think of as a mainstream classic was once considered not only a risk, but a play of low character and dubious taste – notably when Mrs Hardcastle falls into the horse pond.'

His company, Out of Joint, are staging this delightful masterpiece at the National in repertory with April De Angelis's new play *A Laughing Matter*. This deals with David Garrick's rejection of Goldsmith's play for the Drury Lane Theatre, where he was actor-manager. It's the kind of link that Stafford-Clark enjoys making: during his regime at the Royal Court he famously teamed Farquhar's *The Recruiting Officer* with Timberlake Wertenbaker's *Our Country's Good*, and later Etherege's *The Man of Mode* with Stephen Jeffreys's *The Libertine*. 'I find this kind of dialogue with the past fascinating,' he says. 'The new play invariably illuminates the old play and it's doing so here. April is a writer of great eccentricity and originality, who's always been interested in history. *A Laughing Matter* is not only funny, but a very truthful account of backstage life and the decisions a theatre manager has to take.'

Returning to rehearsal, he gathers the actors round him and offers them some final thoughts about Act four. 'As far as the play has a dark part, this is it,' he explains. 'It's not as riotously funny as the first act, the characters are less confident about who and where they are. All is not quite as they think, so it's more sober. Everyone has to think on the spot, and that's how you should colour it.'

They run part of the act straight through, catching neatly the characters' various confusions. 'My boots, ho!' cries Tony Lumpkin finally. And so to lunch.

She Stoops to Conquer opened in the Lyttelton in November 2002.

Mocking the world's follies

John Caird explains why he's directing a rarely performed nineteenth-century comedy

After *Troilus and Cressida* and *Candide*, the National's new ensemble is tackling a fascinating but little-known Victorian play. Edward Bulwer-Lytton's 'serious comedy' *Money* is a love story, but also a powerful attack on poverty and the complacency of the rich, which manages to be both morally serious and deeply comic. If Bulwer-Lytton is remembered at all today, it's usually for his novels, notably *The Last Days of Pompeii*. But his plays, including *Richelieu* and *The Lady of Lyons*, were regularly performed in the Victorian era. *Money*, written in 1840, was briefly revived at the Other Place in 1982 by the Royal Shakespeare Company.

Talking just before rehearsals begin, John Caird is full of enthusiasm for this spirited play, which he has long wanted to direct. 'What it says is astonishingly accurate about the way money affects people's lives, their relationships and attitudes,' he observes. 'And with the boom in materialism in the last two decades, it's a play that's more relevant to us than ever.' Like Dickens, though from a very different background, Bulwer-Lytton was unhappy about the obscene gap that existed in his day between rich and poor.

'*Money* is a work full of reforming zeal, but it's not a tract,' Caird says. 'There's some wonderfully angry laughter going on underneath, it makes its points very dexterously: Bulwer-Lytton mocks the world and its follies in a way that is very watchable.' His comic characters are reminiscent of those found in the Restoration plays of morality and manners by Wycherley, Congreve and Farquhar – which is no surprise, since Bulwer-Lytton grew up watching those plays. But *Money* also looks forward to the naturalistic late-Victorian works of Arthur Wing Pinero and Henry Arthur Jones. Intriguingly, Gorky, Ibsen and Chekhov were all influenced by Bulwer-Lytton.

Although Caird is setting his production in the play's own period, he's not aiming to pay slavish attention to period detail. 'What I like about *Money* is the almost complete absence of naturalistic clutter in the scenes,' he says. 'It becomes a play free to be dominated by its ideas, by its characters and their motives.' He defends the love scenes between Bulwer-Lytton's hero and heroine against the charge that they are melo-dramatic. 'Alfred Evelyn and Clara Douglas speak to each other in a restrained way because they're obeying the forms of Victorian etiquette. But actually their relationship is passionate and complex, and plagued by misapprehensions caused by money. The scenes may read like melodrama, but they will act really well.'

He believes Simon Russell Beale and Victoria Hamilton are ideal for these two principal roles. 'You need actors who really understand what they're wrestling with, not just romantic-looking people who can give an impersonation of the emotions,' he says. 'It's an ideas play, so you need ideas actors. Both Simon and Victoria are intelligent, and have fine analytical minds. But they're also comedians, which is vital. You need actors who can be absolutely serious, but at the same time tip it just over the edge, so you're laughing at the follies of mankind rather than bewailing them.'

Money opened in the Olivier in June 1999.

Fiona and Bernard go touring

Two Shaws are joining forces for a mobile production of *Widowers' Houses*

Fiona Shaw is both thrilled and frightened at the prospect of directing Bernard Shaw's *Widowers' Houses*. 'God knows why they've asked me, I'm still on the nursery slopes as a director. I'm terrified – but I'm also attracted by the fear. I would never have suggested the idea myself, but that's what makes it rather wonderful.'

Talking after a morning of auditioning actors for the other Shaw's first play, the voluble Irish actress, seen most recently at the National as Jean Brodie, is already fired up by her first directing job on the South Bank, and teeming with ideas for a production that will shortly be seen in many different theatres in England, Wales and Ireland.

It's a bold move by NT Education, to engage her for *Widowers' Houses*, for if she's in her prime as an actress of acknowledged brilliance, her experience of directing is strictly limited. What she calls 'my only joined-up directing work' was on *The Hamlet Project*, with a young company from Dublin's Abbey Theatre. Usefully, this too was a mobile production, which toured around Ireland to many unusual spaces, including a fish factory, a mental asylum and a disused hospital.

As an actress she's worked with some of the best directors in the land, including Phyllida Lloyd, Stephen Daldry and Deborah Warner, and is all too aware of their shadows looming. 'With so much talent around, it's hard not to feel inadequate. All I can do is make the attempt. What I like about directing is that you have to look at the play from everyone's point of view. It gives you a chance to free yourself.' She found it difficult at first to make much sense of *Widowers' Houses*, a play that begins as romantic comedy, then suddenly changes into an angry indictment of landlords who shamelessly exploit the poor.

'It's a pre-Shavian play really, he hasn't yet mastered his ideas about theatre, so he's floundering quite a bit,' she suggests. But a reading at the National's Studio changed her perception of the play. 'I think the secret is that it's much more emotional than it appears to be on the page. As with Ibsen, you need to find the play beneath the play, to get at that godless, unpoetic world where there's a seeming domestic situation, but something much more epic going on underneath.' The play's ostensible subject, the question of rent, is one that she finds it hard to get enthusiastic about. 'Because it's potentially dry, I feel the only wet way in is through the emotional life of the characters,' she observes. 'Shaw's protective tone conceals a much messier underbelly, and a violence hinted at in certain scenes. I look forward to investigating that.'

She confesses to being 'gobsmacked' at the apparent difficulty of creating a set that has to be put up and taken down in two hours, and needs to fit into the hugely different spaces that the production will visit during the twenty-two-venue tour. But she's also excited by the challenge this presents. 'I would have loved to have built an installation, but you can't do that for a tour like this,' she says. 'So at the moment I'm exploring the idea of using organic materials, stones and glass, objects that the actors can play with. I'm hoping the texture will be quite untheatrical: no library bookshelves or anything like that.'

Widowers' Houses, which was first performed in 1892, has been somewhat neglected since then. When Fiona meets Bernard, the result could be a collector's item. 'The play is very untypical of his work, and the less typical I can make it the better,' she says. 'I shall be deconstructing it within an inch of its life.'

Widowers' Houses toured from October 1999 to February 2000.

Echoes and influences

Peter Gill reflects on his timely revival of
The Voysey Inheritance

When Harley Granville Barker's play was first staged at the Court Theatre in 1905, it was hailed as a masterpiece of the new drama. A century later, director Peter Gill believes it has more than stood the test of time. 'Outside Shakespeare, I believe it ranks with anything in the theatrical canon,' he says, as we talk during rehearsals. 'I thought it an astonishing play when I first saw it, and I think it even more so now I'm working on it for the National.'

The central story of *The Voysey Inheritance*, with its echoes of *Hamlet*, concerns Edward Voysey's efforts to deal with the consequences of his father's corruption. Mr Voysey, a well-respected lawyer, has for years been cheating his clients by secretly and successfully speculating with their capital. Having revealed his shady dealings to his son, who is also his partner, he dies. This leaves Edward struggling with his principles as he tries to decide whether or not to carry on with the fraud.

The play established Granville Barker as one of the foremost dramatists of his time, on a par with Shaw. But he also achieved fame as an actor, a manager, a ground-breaking Shakespearean director, a theatrical innovator, and the moving spirit behind the campaign for a National Theatre. Peter Gill speaks warmly about his influence and achievement. 'He was the first in the British theatre to have the idea of a repertory company. The notion of a serious theatre, with all the component parts coming together, rather than some kind of director's version of the actor-manager. It's what George Devine tried to do in the 1950s and 1960s, also at the Royal Court.'

He believes *The Voysey Inheritance* is Granville Barker's best play. 'I've read all his others recently, and although *Waste* and *The Madras House* are extraordinary, I think this is his finest achievement. It's more than just a play about one man's dealing with his father's fraudulent legacy: it's also a portrait of a comfortable section of the upper-middle class, the professional classes, the administrators of empire, that Granville Barker captures brilliantly.'

Like Granville Barker, Gill started out as an actor. He, too, is an acclaimed playwright, his plays including *Cardiff East*, *Small Change* and *The York Realist*. He has also been an influential figure within British theatre generally, first as an associate director of the Royal Court, then as the founder director of Riverside Studios, and later as an associate director of the National and founding director of its Studio.

As someone who has also adapted *The Cherry Orchard* and *The Seagull*, he has found echoes of the great Russian dramatist in *The Voysey Inheritance*. 'It's almost Chekhovian in the way Granville Barker keeps fifteen characters in play,' he suggests. 'It's a wonderfully composed play, moving as it does between sustained duologues and group scenes. It's most diligently made and yet brilliant.'

At a moment when corruption and scandal have returned to the centre of British politics, a new production of a powerful play about clandestine financial skulduggery could hardly be more timely. Inevitably there have been conversations in rehearsals about relevant current events. But as Gill is keen to point out, *The Voysey Inheritance* is not essentially a piece of political theatre. 'It's not a Shavian play, it's not a tract, it's a much more deeply explored portrait of a particular group of people. You never quite know what Granville Barker's politics are. But the play has a resolute poetic truthfulness. It's well written without being deliberately aphoristic, it's a poetic play without poeticisms.'

He's delighted with the casting of the National's production, which stars Dominic West as Edward Voysey and Nancy Carroll as Alice Maitland, and Julian Glover playing Mr Voysey. 'Dominic has a wonderfully warm, confident and demonstrative quality, which very much suits how Edward turns out in the end. Nancy is a fascinating, unusual actress, stylish but natural, who identifies easily with the bold kind of young woman that Alice is. And Julian has just the right blend of power, authority and humour to play the buccaneering Mr Voysey. I'm very lucky to have them.'

Rehearsals, he says, have been satisfying. 'The text of the play is very dense and the wonderful duologues are quite long. So it's time-consuming work, but very rewarding. The number and the complexity of the relationships mean you find something new in it every day.'

Doubts and uncertainties

Dominic West on getting inside Edward Voysey's mind

There are certain challenges to playing Edward. You start the play at an intense emotional pitch. The bottom has just fallen out of his world. He's just discovered that the father he adores and respects is a fraud and a cheat. It's the horrible disappointment of the child when he first realises his parents are fallible.

It reminds me of Biff Loman in *Death of a Salesman*, but there are countless examples in drama. Few, however, start the play by walking on stage and bursting into tears. Granville Barker wrote a similar high jump for a character I once acted in his play *Waste*: walk on, crack up. It doesn't give the actor much to work off, but it immediately kicks the play into gear.

What follows is the journey from innocence to experience; the journey many of us make from rebellion against our parents, to becoming just like them. Except that, unlike his father, Edward's integrity remains intact at the end of the play. His high moral stance emerges battered but uncompromised and, in losing his priggish hauteur, he gets the girl as well. Alice won't take him until he's lost some of his purity. So the damning inheritance becomes a blessing in disguise. Had Edward not had to 'face the music' he'd never have won Alice.

Edward's rectitude was a key problem for me initially, not having a great deal of it myself. His outrage at his father's crime is a professional as well as a personal one. Financial impropriety isn't really what gets my blood boiling. Nick Leeson or Enron don't excite the same visceral reaction that Gary Glitter does; even when one considers that people are 'beggared' by their greed. So I found it hard to feel the passion of Edward's professional indignation.

I talked to the Head of Finance at the National, and asked her if the crime Mr Voysey commits – speculating on a client's capital and pocketing the interest, while paying the client's ordinary rate of interest – would be considered a crime today. It seemed to me to be what banks do all the time. She said, 'Absolutely, that's embezzlement. It's the worst thing someone in his position could do.' And I began to see, as Edward does, that poverty and social injustice begin with the subtle corruptions of 'nice' men like Mr Voysey.

I have wanted to work with Peter Gill for some time. He has an unusual degree of empathy for actors, probably because he used to be one. He also brings the skills of a writer and an incisive social commentator to bear. He has an extraordinary breadth of knowledge and a great skill in contextualising things: you ask a question about your character and you get a brilliant one-minute precis of the Franco-Prussian War. To my mind, he knows more about British theatre than anyone alive.

Morals and principles

Nancy Carroll on playing Alice Maitland

The play appealed to me immediately; it has an almost epic quality to it. Granville Barker uses many characters to tell his story, which is so delicately woven. I like the fact that the play doesn't have a definite message, he doesn't spell out his moral view – which is a relief. I think that appeals to a modern audience. He allows us to digest the story at our own rate and draw our own conclusions, gently empowering us.

In several plays written around this time there was a surge towards creating a slightly more 'real' woman. Shaw is the obvious example: his women are often strong-minded characters in their own right. Women had tended to be representational. They had represented an emotional state or a moral slant, usually with regard to a more central male character.

Alice certainly has an element of the Shavian woman, but she is perhaps less political and more grounded. Whatever we decide about the principles of Edward's final decision, Alice allows him to be himself. He is able to express himself to her, without the emotional complications that make him stumble within his own family. She seems to be a beacon of honesty for Edward, which makes her a joy to play.

We have assumed that the Voysey family expect Alice and Edward to marry eventually. He has proposed to her four and a half times and she has so far refused him. Her strength is that she could survive without him, but their journey is a very interesting and lovely one, and her devotion to him slowly unravels.

Beatrice, Edward's sister-in-law, and Alice are the boldest and most forward-thinking of the women. And yet, fundamentally, they want their men to be 'men' – in the true romantic-hero sense of the word. Alice at last accepts Edward when he becomes this 'man'. Finally he takes the situation by the short and curlies without adhering to what is sensibly right or wrong.

It's interesting to compare this play with one of Shaw's. I've just finished playing Gloria Clandon in *You Never Can Tell* in the West End. I often felt I was trying to breathe life into a very literary version of what Shaw thought the character should say, rather than what a young Edwardian woman would say. Very generally, his characters don't seem as rounded as Granville Barker's do. In *The Voysey Inheritance* he has created people with a depth of complexity and a humanity and joy, who are only a pleasure to explore and play.

The Voysey Inheritance opened in the Lyttelton in April 2006.

Duelling personality

Ian McKellen on the joys and agonies of playing Captain Hook in *Peter Pan*

J. M. Barrie's seemingly immortal play *Peter Pan* has some very particular resonances for Ian McKellen. To begin with, it was the first play he ever saw in a theatre. He remembers that Captain Hook was his favourite part. But more significantly, it strikes some deep chords in someone who suffered a tragic loss when he was a boy.

'My mother died when I was twelve, and every time I see the play I find it plucks at heartstrings of regret in me,' he confesses. 'I was a boy who never really had a mother. I had nightmares about what had happened to her. Was she locked up somewhere? Why had she left me? With this play, in which Barrie keeps asking what a mother is, he is exploring something very potent – not just for me, but for other Lost Boys.'

Taking a break in rehearsals at the National, McKellen's momentary sombreness in recalling his early loss vanishes as he remembers his first taste of *Peter Pan*, a touring production in Manchester, which he saw at the tender age of three. 'It could have put me off theatre for life, going that young,' he says. 'I could see the wires, so the flying had no enchantment for me. The starlight wasn't very well done either; I suspect it was a very tacky show. What fooled me totally was the dog, which I thought was real. But generally I wasn't very impressed: the train journey from Wigan was much more exciting.'

It's this formative experience that clearly lies behind his strongly expressed belief that *Peter Pan* is essentially a play for adults – especially in the case of the current version by John Caird and Trevor Nunn, staged in an earlier production by the Royal Shakespeare Company, in which the Lost Boys are played by twenty-something actors. 'Although generations of kids have been to it, I think it is an odd play to take them to; I suspect they don't enjoy it as much as their parents do. On the other hand it does have some magical moments of great simplicity, which couldn't work on film and don't work fully in the novel.' He's sceptical too about those who read deep psychological meanings into the tradition of one actor playing both Hook and Mr Darling, supposedly representing the Good and Evil in all of us. 'I think that's read into it and not helpful at all for an actor. After all, it was Gerald du Maurier's idea and Barrie was indifferent to it, as he was to the idea of a girl playing Peter.'

In tackling the two roles McKellen is following in some notable theatrical footsteps. After du Maurier in the original 1904 production, those who have done the double act include Charles Laughton, Ralph Richardson, Donald Wolfit, Donald Sinden and Joss Ackland. Only Alastair Sim declined the Darling role. Barrie wanted Captain Hook to terrify the audience, but the part obviously has comic possibilities too. McKellen is finding that both elements are emerging as he develops the character. 'I find myself sounding rather like Donald Sinden at times, which makes it both funny and sinister.'

But he is less interested in the funny or scary debate about Hook than in whether a character whom Barrie describes as 'one of a different class from his crew, a solitary among uncultured companions' will be really understood by younger members of the audience. 'The play is nearly a hundred years old,' he observes. 'I wonder what a modern child will make of this Old Etonian who's fallen on hard times, or maybe cast himself out of society? Will he know what Good Form is? Will they understand the meaning of Hook's last line, Floreat Etona? Of course they won't.'

Although he's clearly beginning to enjoy himself in the role of Peter Pan's duelling partner, he's keen to emphasise that shows which audiences find charming and delightful, such as *Peter Pan* and *The Wind in the Willows*, can impose huge physical demands on the actors. 'My friends say, "You must be having such fun doing Hook." And I say, "Oh yes? A ridiculous black wig, a very uncomfortable costume, only able to use one arm, forever hanging upside down, going down tunnels, fighting duels, jumping into lagoons, risking breaking an ankle – where is the fun in that?" And I don't even get to fly.'

Peter Pan opened in the Olivier in December 1997.

Shaw the even-handed modernist

Marianne Elliott on the many virtues of *Saint Joan*

When I read the play I was stunned by what an amazing woman Joan was. Shaw says she is the female equivalent of Hamlet, and it's true. She's struggling with massive life and philosophical choices, and what it means to do the right thing. But unlike Hamlet she's very young. Her life is short, fast and furious, and it changes the course of history.

The joy of her is that she has so many different sides: visionary, warrior, peasant girl. Luckily records were kept of the trial, because she was such a celebrity. We have a lot of information about this girl who lived in the 1400s, and Shaw was able to make direct use of the transcripts in the trial scene.

If you're interested in ideas and debate there's a huge amount in the play, regardless of whether you're religious. It's a fascinating piece, because it swings from left to right all the time. Shaw keeps you on your toes, so you're not sure where your sympathies lie. It's not obvious what you're meant to think or feel: he's very even-handed and fair. He didn't want there to be villains hounding a pure white virgin who is godly and divine, he wanted to make it more human.

Sometimes with period pieces audiences feel alienated and think, 'That happened then, but what has it to do with me?' That's not what Shaw wanted, and that's why he wrote the play in very modern, colloquial language. He's making us look at ourselves and say, 'If Joan were alive today, would we hound her to death in the same way?' She's a rebel, and in his view a rebel is not a derogatory term.

The original play is quite long, so we've cut it here and there. Shaw was a raconteur, a fantastic debater and public speaker, who used all sorts of methods to make his points. He was also quite loquacious and often went round the houses to make them. We've just cut a few of those houses and also trimmed the Epilogue while keeping its essential argument.

Joan is a very demanding role for an actress; she's only off stage for one scene. I think Anne-Marie has all the elements needed. She's got the youth and the energy, there's something tough and streetwise about her, but she's also very appealing, so one warms to her as a person. She was our first choice for the part.

Playing a firebrand

Anne-Marie Duff on taking on Shaw's feisty heroine

The first thing that struck me about the play was how relevant it is today. That's the interesting thing about a writer like Shaw: his plays are full of similar themes, but they're all so different. *Saint Joan* is a visceral play, with a very different flavour from his others.

Ten years ago, when I played Cordelia in *King Lear* at the National, Richard Eyre told me to think about Saint Joan as a kind of model. I suppose there are similarities: they both are on a crusade, have a strong sense of doing right, and are completely uncompromising in a self-righteous way. But Joan is a real firebrand and I found that very exciting. She's an incredibly strong young woman, with so many different qualities, which is great for an actor, because it gives you so much to work with. She's a champion and we need champions. Sometimes they turn into despots and maniacs, but she never did that.

I suppose actors usually share some characteristics with the person they're playing. I can certainly relate to Joan's tenacity, her drive and her ambition. I'm also drawn to characters that have a real commitment to an idea, who throw themselves up against it and end up a bit bruised.

Joan's language is very juicy, but it has an epic as well as a colloquial quality, which adds to her peculiarity and separation from the rest of the world. I find her speeches very beautiful and incredibly moving; they're fiery and inciting, but also really tender and poetic, which is not something you normally connect with Shaw.

During rehearsals we've all done masses of research. There are many brilliant books about Joan, which tell you about the war, what she was born into, what shaped her, what was happening at the time the voices first came to her, or when she left home. They help to take her out of the book of saints that you had when you were a kid.

We've also thought a lot about territory, relating it to current situations such as that in Palestine. We live in a world full of young martyrs. What's the difference between Joan and them? The play brings up lots of such questions, which is fascinating: I like having that kind of debate going on in my head.

Saint Joan opened in the Olivier in June 2007.

European Drama

The power of shyness

Charlotte Rampling on Marivaux's
The False Servant and her new theatre career

It's a surprise to discover that an actress with such a glittering film career as Charlotte Rampling's had never worked in the theatre until a few months ago. 'I just thought it was time to bite the bullet,' she says, talking shortly before rehearsals for *The False Servant* begin. 'I felt ready for the challenge, I just wanted to be out there.' Now, after making her debut in France last year, she's poised to play the Countess in Marivaux's witty and cynical play at the National.

Having been partly educated in France and lived there most of her life, she's fluent in French and very much at home in the culture. Yet she hesitated before agreeing to appear in *Petits Crimes Conjugaux*, a two-hander about marital breakdown, which played in Paris in the winter. 'It was a very combative part, which required an enormous range of emotion,' she recalls, 'and I was on stage for the whole ninety minutes. It took some time before I understood the process. Partly it was the sheer novelty of it, but I also had to concentrate on my French pronunciation, and on making sure I was heard in that 750-seat theatre. But once it got going it was fine.'

In her youth she did a year's training at the Royal Court Theatre School, in the Theatre Upstairs. But her film career took off early, initially in British films such as *The Knack* and *Georgy Girl*. Once she settled in France and became a star of the European cinema, she says it proved too complicated to accept the occasional theatre offer that came her way. But there was another obstacle. 'I felt quite shy about being on stage, and when you see other actors doing so much, you get more and more so. I'll always be shy, but I think that's possibly an advantage, because when you're acting you need to dominate that shyness, and that can make you more powerful.'

She saw a production of *The False Servant* in France fifteen years ago, starring Jane Birkin, so was thrilled when director Jonathan Kent made her an offer and sent her Martin Crimp's translation. 'I read it alongside the French version. It's very funny and very modern, and says a lot of truths about society and the way we live.' Marivaux's Countess is rather different from the cool, often mysterious characters she has tended to play on screen. Yet until she starts rehearsing she's reluctant to talk about her role.

'I need to be with the other actors before her character emerges. I make my choices on gut instinct, then I find the character jumps out at you and grabs you. It's like a magic spell: you leave it to mature for a while, and it blossoms and grows.' She hopes to do more theatre in the future, while continuing with her film career. 'Doing both kinds of work is a fabulously beautiful rhythm for an actress.'

The False Servant opened in the Cottesloe in May 2004.

Exposing the human beast

Marianne Elliott on Emile Zola's dark and compelling *Thérèse Raquin*

Six years after it was published in 1867, Emile Zola turned his popular novel *Thérèse Raquin* into a play. Although its structure is very good, many of the elements are unsophisticated. The play is quite straightforward, while the book is hugely rich, detailed and multifaceted. So Nicholas Wright and I, in adapting his translation for this production, have tried to get some of the complexity of the book into the play.

It's a very dark work, and very brave and forward-thinking for the time, before Freud and psychoanalysis became part of our everyday language. Zola was interested in the human beast. It's unearthed a lot of the dark side in us, the things that we don't really like to look at, such as infidelity, uncontrollable desires, hatred and murder. It's really fascinating in terms of the psychology of the characters.

There's a strong sense of inevitability in the story. Given Camille's temperament and mindset, it's inevitable that Thérèse and Laurent do what they do. And it's equally inevitable that, although they're not religious or moralistic, they're traumatised by their action. It's very compelling, like a ball that gathers and gathers and gathers moss. Thérèse is quite an enigmatic, ghostly, disturbing figure. Zola sets up a world in which as far as she's concerned she is treated quite abominably: she's completely stifled, like that girl they've just found in Vienna, and not allowed any individuality. It's assumed she'll marry Camille, the very first man she met, who is in effect her brother, and of course it's a disaster.

We thought about taking it out of the period, but then a lot of the plot wouldn't work. For example, if we set it in more modern times, Thérèse and Laurent could leave, or Thérèse could get divorced, whereas in the nineteenth century they have no alternative to their action – at least they think they don't have. So we're keeping it in period, but trying to make them as modern as possible, rather than characters in a museum piece.

Thérèse Raquin opened in the Lyttelton in November 2006.

Eternal truths

Why does Ibsen's rarely performed *An Enemy of the People* seem so modern? What does Ian McKellen make of the motives of its protagonist?

Ibsen's vibrant and stirring play has had a peculiarly chequered stage history. Before last year's production by Trevor Nunn at the National, which has now returned to the repertoire, there have (not counting an adaptation by Arthur Miller) been only three productions in London during the twentieth century.

Part of the reason for this comparative neglect clearly lies in the play's cast of twenty-six characters, which makes it expensive and difficult to stage. But in a time of universal suffrage its appeal has perhaps lessened because of the ideas expressed by Ibsen's protagonist Dr Stockmann, especially his illiberal belief that 'the majority is always wrong'.

Yet Ibsen's biographer Michael Meyer, a shrewd critic of his work, had no doubts about the play's timeless qualities. 'It is the first political debate which succeeds in remaining a great play,' he wrote in 1967. 'The truths it expresses have not dated, and are not likely to as long as there are town councils and politicians.' Those truths concern the connections between their private interests and public morality, together with Ibsen's attacks on political corruption and the squalid ethics of newspaper journalism. It requires little imagination to see how these issues, all bound up in a story of environmental pollution and attempts to cover it up, resonate powerfully with today's audiences.

The story concerns Tomas Stockmann, a doctor in a small Norwegian spa town, who discovers that the baths that attract visitors to it are contaminated with bacteria. At first he is praised for publicly exposing the health risk, but as the townsfolk gradually realise how their livelihoods will be affected if the truth is revealed, they turn against him. In contrast to the dark, claustrophobic psychological family dramas such as *Ghosts* and *Hedda Gabler*, *An Enemy of the People* is very much a public play, notably in the famous fourth act, in which Ibsen's hero harangues the townsfolk for their cowardice, ignorance and stupidity, and is made an outcast.

Ibsen wrote the play at much greater speed than usual, fired up by the virulently hostile reception given to his previous play, *Ghosts*. ('Morbid, unhealthy, unwholesome, disgusting' and 'an open drain' were representative comments from London critics.) Many of his protagonist's scornful views about the masses are Ibsen's own: 'Dr Stockmann and I got on most excellently; we agree about so many things,' he wrote to his publisher.

The play has aroused emotions and ignited controversy in

very different contexts. In 1905 in Russia it became the favourite play of the revolutionaries, who admired Stockmann for boldly standing up for 'the truth'. During the run of the Moscow Art Theatre's production in Petrograd the play was subject to political censorship and the company expected arrests to be made nightly. Stanislavsky, who was playing Dr Stockmann, records the audience's reaction at a moment of great political ferment: 'My words aroused such pandemonium we had to stop the performance . . . The entire audience rose from their seats and hurled themselves towards the footlights . . . The younger people jumped on to the stage and embraced Dr Stockmann.'

In 1950 Arthur Miller adapted the play during the notorious McCarthyite witch-hunt against communism, relating it to 'the need, if not the holy right, to resist the pressure to conform'. Inevitably he got into trouble with some critics, who detected anti-US propaganda in certain lines (which were in fact Ibsen's own). 'Nothing would burn off the fog of suspicion that I had used Ibsen as a front for the Reds,' he recalled.

Miller confessed to being uncomfortable about the anti-democratic and unashamedly elitist views of Ibsen's hero. But today this is often seen as a strength of the play, since it makes Stockmann something rather more complicated and interesting than just a champion of 'the truth'. Christopher Hampton, who has provided a superbly colloquial and fluent translation for the National production, is one who takes this line, suggesting: 'Ibsen is too subtle and profound a dramatist not to know that there are few figures more infuriating than the man who is always right.'

An Enemy of the People clearly has the potential to reach out to audiences of all kinds. As Michael Meyer suggested, 'Even when only adequately performed, it is one of the most accessible and compelling of Ibsen's plays, and Dr Stockmann is one of the greatest male parts he wrote.' Trevor Nunn's powerful and fluid production has fully exploited that accessibility, using the Olivier revolve to open the play out into the bustling town, and making ingenious use of parts of the auditorium for the celebrated public meeting scene.

Ian McKellen's performance as Stockmann is certainly never less than compelling. His scintillating portrait of a man driven to near-insanity by a combustible mixture of emotions and principles has been justly hailed as a great performance.

Ian McKellen on Dr Stockmann

I think the play is just as much a family story, a tussle between two brothers, as it is one about the individual fighting an oppressive authority. Dr Stockmann says he is trying to clean up society. But isn't his motive as much to get his own back on his brother, who has been very successful in life, as it is to stand up for a principle?

What makes people want to make a fuss? Is it that they actually enjoy doing so, or do they feel duty bound to make a point whatever it costs them? That's what makes the play interesting for me. What are people who go into public life really like? What are their real motives? How far can they be trusted? These are issues the play throws up.

To stand up and speak the truth like Dr Stockmann does take bravery, but it's a bravery that goes hand in hand with foolishness and arrogance. Might it not have been better, for instance, for him to have written back to the laboratory and asked them if there was some way to combat the poison? Chlorine hadn't been discovered then: perhaps he should have spent his time discovering it! There are all sorts of ways in which you can deal with the truth, and shouting is only one of them.

An Enemy of the People opened in the Olivier in September 1997.

Going for the epic

Marianne Elliott on directing *Pillars of the Community*, Ibsen's first real prose drama

With its huge cast and difficult ending, *Pillars of the Community* is on the face of it a very hard play to do. But it's also a very rich one and utterly surprising. Everyone knows what *A Doll's House* and *Hedda Gabler* are about, but *Pillars of the Community* is not at all what you'd expect from Ibsen.

In the first place it's very funny; there's a lot of comedy in the first three acts. It's also structured like a thriller, and very compelling in the way thrillers are. There are shifts and turns all the time, so you're always wondering what's going to happen next. The surprises happen for the audience and the characters at the same time, and Ibsen is constantly pulling the rug from under your feet. It's quite obviously relevant for today, because it's about a man who bases his life and career and a huge amount of fame on lies, and about the people who buy those lies, because they're very important to them. It's modern because it's about a well-known public figure apologising for his actions and announcing his fallibility, possibly getting away with it, and rebirthing himself as something else. It's also very up to date, because it's about a capitalist society in which people are obsessed by greed and the pursuit of wealth.

I'm fascinated by the way it talks a lot about America. It's set in the 1870s, and some of the characters believe that America is the land of the free, a place where people are allowed to be themselves. They see it as a place to escape to, away from the repression that characterises the small town in Norway where they live. It's beautifully ironic, it's like when a Chekhov character says, 'For future generations everything will be much better' – whereas we know it isn't.

We're not doing the play in a naturalistic way. I wanted to get away from a lot of Ibsen productions I've seen, which tend to be set in the drawing room, with antimacassars and too many pictures on the wall. All those choices by the director are perfectly understandable and right, but I wanted to do something a little more epic, because to me the play feels quite large-scale, almost operatic. Within the play there are people lurking in shadows, overhearing things they shouldn't be hearing, and intercepting letters. I thought it would be interesting therefore to give it a kind of *film noir* aesthetic, with people being lit in and out of the shadows. So we've placed the action in a cinemascope shape in a very large room, where the walls then start peeling away, enabling you to see the machinations happening outside the house and people overhearing things from behind the doors.

There are a lot of elements to overcome and that's exciting. The better-known plays are hermetically sealed and polished. This one is less so, because Ibsen was using it to experiment with matters such as structure and form, colloquial dialogue and ideas such as the emancipation of women. It was the beginning of a journey for him.

When it came to casting the two main parts, Damian Lewis seemed to me an ideal Bernick. He has an incredible amount of charm and charisma, you can see him as the person all the women in the community are going to be in love with, and the one all the men would like to be. He's got a sort of ease about him, which will enable him to stand out in this very stiff and proper community. Lona is a difficult part to play. I wanted someone who would have an empathy with Bernick's character, but also would be convincing at putting the boot in with wit and power. Lesley Manville fits the bill perfectly.

Exposing the truth

Lesley Manville on playing a lesser-known Ibsen heroine

Lona Hessel is a feminist and a fantastic character to play. At the time Ibsen wrote *Pillars of the Community* the women's movement had been going for more than forty years in America. The influences were gradually coming over to Europe. All over the place women were popping up who were seeking equality on a domestic and social level, as well as a religious one. The movement was just kicking into action in Norway when Ibsen came to write the play.

In the eyes of the town Lona is the black sheep of the family, this dreadful woman who actually dared to leave the community and go to that evil place called America. Then she returns home, to this atmosphere of doom and gloom, darkness and suppression, and blows the whole place open in her determination to expose the truth about the town's leading citizen, Bernick.

She's a very strong and independent woman, highly critical and sarcastic, and invariably on the attack. The challenge for me is to find other layers and levels in her character beyond her aggression. Damian and I have been able to do this through exploring the subtext in our scenes together. We're making it clear that Lona wants to help Bernick, and although she's determined to make him see the error of his ways, she can sometimes do so in a tender manner. The lines can be played in many ways.

It may sound surprising, but I find the play rather similar to Chekhov in certain respects. I've acted in *The Cherry Orchard* and *Three Sisters*, and like them, *Pillars of the Community* is often more about what isn't said than what is. I wasn't familiar with it before, but I do think it's a great play about the human condition – the minutiae of our lives. What I find truly staggering is the resonance that it has for today's world, what it says about the lives and behaviour of public figures. To take a recent example, George Bush's apology for his failure to cope with the New Orleans disaster is reminiscent of the ending of the play, where you have Bernick apologising for his misdeeds, but using it as a political device to protect his career.

I think Samuel Adamson has done a particularly good adaptation. He's made it easier to speak the lines than some of the earlier versions. He's changed certain things to make aspects of the play clearer, but he's done it very subtly. Ibsen had been struggling for some time to find a new language that was realistic, and felt he had achieved it with *Pillars of the Community*. If he were around today, I think he would be very moved by this version.

Pillars of the Community opened in the Lyttelton in October 2005.

161

Connections and echoes

Ben Whishaw sees Hamlet as a good preparation for playing Konstantin in Chekhov's *The Seagull*

I always played character roles at drama school. I never thought I'd be cast in leading parts. When I auditioned for Trevor Nunn's Old Vic production of *Hamlet*, I though I was going up for a Guard, or at best Rosencrantz or Guildenstern. To play Hamlet himself was an absolute joy from start to finish. It was also a good preparation for *The Seagull*. There are all sorts of connections and echoes between the two characters: at one point Konstantin even quotes Hamlet. But what attracted me initially was the play, which is so brilliantly observed, and the chance to work with Katie Mitchell.

We spent the whole first week of rehearsal on Konstantin's own play, exploring the different theatrical movements that might have inspired it and trying to find a style for it. When you read his play it seems risible, so we wanted to get inside his head to find out what he was trying to do. It's still early in rehearsals, so I'm only just getting to grips with his character, and working with Juliet Stevenson as Arkadina. But playing anyone in an extreme emotional place is always interesting, as well as challenging. It's a great opportunity.

Katie's production of *Three Sisters* at the National blew me away, and I've also admired her *Uncle Vanya* and *Ivanov*. When she directs Chekhov she somehow strips away everything the plays have become encrusted with over the years. She makes these foreign people seem very familiar. I love the meticulousness of her work, its uncompromising nature, the kind of intensity she can create. She's a real artist.

The Seagull opened in the Lyttelton in June 2006.

Poetic but earthy

Stephen Rea on playing the title role in
Cyrano de Bergerac

Although both Antony Sher and Robert Lindsay have recently played Cyrano, I've never seen it done on stage – although I have seen the two film versions, with José Ferrer and Gérard Depardieu. It's a massively romantic role, but it's not soppy or sentimental, it's very real and hard, and that appeals to me a great deal.

I think Depardieu felt too sorry for himself, and I don't want to do that. Cyrano himself says: 'There's nothing uglier than a tear that flows, down the grim length of a ridiculous nose.' It's a great line in itself and that to me is the key to the whole thing: he wouldn't give way to sentimentality about himself. I also think he can be quite cruel. I've tried to emphasise that he can be fairly ruthless in the duel. Sometimes it's fudged that he kills the man, but it's clear that at that moment he decides to punish the world because of his affliction. He wouldn't be human if he didn't.

For the play to be tragic, which in the end it is, the flip side is that it's terribly funny, so I hope we can get that element too. I'd like very much to feel I'm not just approaching this classical piece to test myself against other greater performances. I want to throw the play up in the air a bit, so it's a bit more relaxed. That's the beauty of a modern, Irish way of doing it.

Derek Mahon's new version is very distinctive. It's more poetic than earlier ones, which is not surprising, since it's written by a great Irish poet. I think poets have great courage; they take language somewhere new, they carve out spaces for us. And Derek definitely does that – of all the Irish poets I would say he does that most. He comes from a mile up the road from me in Belfast, so I have sympathy with his writing anyway. His version is fantastic, it has a voice I find very attractive. It's quite direct in lots of ways and very earthy, and more comic than usual.

In rehearsals we've been finding ways of doing things that

aren't so traditional. It's a matter of how you do it, rather than finding any new aspects in the characters. We don't want the play to have a heavy period feel, so we've set it at the time when Rostand was writing, at the end of the nineteenth century, rather than in the time of the musketeers. We're trying to liberate it from that image of musketeerland, when a part of people's minds closes down, because they feel they've seen it before.

In some respects the play has similarities with Boucicault's *The Shaughraun*, which I did at the National in 1988. I do think that was one of the most exciting Olivier productions. Some woman wrote to me during the run saying: 'This is what theatre was before the intellectuals got hold of it.' I sort of know what she meant, because your only responsibility when you were seeing it was to have a good time. Of course it wasn't without its political edge: the stage Irishman had been a figure of fun in Victorian theatre, and what Boucicault did was make the Irishman the smartest figure on the stage.

Rostand would have been almost a contemporary of Boucicault, the theatre conventions would have a similarity, so they would understand each other. But that's as far as it goes. We're not trying to repeat ourselves: *The Shaughraun* is not an Irish *Cyrano de Bergerac*. But something of the approach will be similar. Why *The Shaughraun* worked in the Olivier is that it had a very direct contact with the audience. The plays that struggle there are the ones where the audience is not as fully acknowledged. I think we'll be able to play off them again.

Cyrano de Bergerac opened in the Olivier in April 2004.

Playing an enigma

Eve Best considers her role as one of Chekhov's *Three Sisters*

Eve Best is excited to be rehearsing *Three Sisters*. 'You can't help being aware of its history and that it's one of the most brilliant plays ever written. You have to treat it with enormous respect and integrity, and be as rigorous as possible. But it's such an exquisitely constructed text, with so much going on underneath, that each scene offers endless possible ways of doing it. And because Chekhov only shows you the tip of the iceberg, so many of them seem to work.'

Her role of Masha has been played by many other fine actresses, including Joan Plowright, Harriet Walter and Sinead Cusack, not to mention Chekhov's wife Olga Knipper, the original in Stanislavsky's 1901 production in Moscow. Yet though there were several productions in the 1990s, the play has not been staged at the National since Olivier's acclaimed 1967 production. 'Masha is an enigma, she's hard to pin down because she behaves in so many different ways,' Best suggests. 'She's tough one moment and vulnerable the next; she can be slow and quick, icy and fiery. But although she's in black, I don't feel she's depressed – quite the opposite. She wants to deal with life, to confront it. She's the one who's always challenging life to a duel.'

In rehearsal director Katie Mitchell has encouraged the actors to improvise. They have played various games, including a nineteenth-century version of Blind Man's Buff, with everyone in character as ten-year-olds. But mostly they have improvised as their adult characters, trying to imagine how they would react in situations outside the play. 'The play is a tiny snippet of what happens over four years,' Best points out. 'We've tried to work out our characters' lives for the rest of the time, so that when we do a scene from the play it's just a logical extension of that. But it's not easy work, because what you invent mustn't go against the text.'

An older sister in real life, she's found these exercises have helped her understand Masha's problem as a middle sister. 'I became conscious for the first time of what a lonely position it can be: because you don't have a role like the oldest or youngest does, you try to find something to make yourself different. So Masha plays the piano possibly to get her father's attention; she gets married before her older sister Olga, so she can say, "At last I'm first at something."' One conclusion she has reached, which Chekhov doesn't refer to, is that for some reason she's unable to have children. 'If she could she would have done, because at that time she could not have refused her husband sex, at least in the early period of their marriage. So again she's deprived of a role, that of a mother.'

Working alongside Lorraine Ashbourne as Olga and Anna Maxwell Martin as Irina, she admires Katie Mitchell's approach to a play that demands top-quality ensemble playing. 'She's brilliant at inspiring a communal feeling, at keeping every single person alive in the rehearsal room. And I find it's a different dynamic working with a woman director: I feel less shy about talking.'

Three Sisters opened in the Lyttelton in July 2003.

Radical and extraordinary

Katie Mitchell has been working with Caryl Churchill on her version of Strindberg's *A Dream Play*

Why did you decide to direct this very difficult play?
The National's director, Nicholas Hytner, wanted to do a production to link up with the exhibition of Strindberg's paintings, drawings and photographs at Tate Modern, and invited me to direct the play of my choice in the Cottesloe. I'd done a couple of productions of *Easter*, one in England and one in Sweden. I prefer later Strindberg, I find the earlier plays too misogynistic.

I think *A Dream Play* is impossibly difficult, but it's the big one and I felt I might never have another chance to have a go at it. Mainly I do fourth-wall realism, which is about behaviour. But that isn't representing what it's like to be inside someone's consciousness. So the challenge of representing someone's dreams, of one dream that one person has, and constructing it in such a way that the audience will really feel they are watching a dream, was just so tantalising and gorgeous.

How did Caryl Churchill come to write your version?
I'd been doing some research into neuro-science, the relationship between the biology of the brain and acting. I mentioned this to Caryl and she'd started to attend some of the workshops. So when I began work on the play she was the one I asked. At first she said no, and I started to waver over my choice of text. But a month later she rang and said, 'I really like the play and I'd like to do it.' And then during a period of two months we discussed it as she drafted it, although of course she did most of the work.

Her version is very different from earlier ones: not just modern, but shorter, and with no supernatural framework involving the gods. Why is that?
That first scene of Agnes coming down to earth was added much later by Strindberg, I think for narrative clarity. It was a very big decision to remove the Eastern religion, but it was actually very inaccurate, so it could have been quite insulting for a modern audience. For example, Indra doesn't have a daughter. So what at the time would have been radical and exciting, when no one would have been very informed about it, could now be disrespectful – and also, we thought, a bit 1970s.

A lot of the religion is now 'backgrounded'. Agnes is someone from another world – we make her very specifically an angel, who has wings, though not all the time. But there is a gap between Caryl's text and what we're now doing. We've made even more radical decisions: we've cut some material, inserted improvisation material, added our own framework of the waking world, and chosen one of the characters to be the dreamer. So the Banker has become a Broker. We see him in his unhappy life, we see him fall asleep, have this very long dream, then wake up. I think this makes the story more accessible. Otherwise it could confuse and frustrate the audience; people will think it's a play and try to put it together, and it won't fit. Once you say there is a waking world and now he's fallen asleep, it will help people not to be alienated from the material.

Your version doesn't always tell us where we are in the kind of detail that Strindberg indicated in his stage directions.

Caryl worked from a literal translation and her version is very close to Strindberg. I think perhaps other translations are not that faithful, they're quite interpretative and add more words than the Swedish, or change it.

How much influence did you have on the text while she was putting it together?

She showed me drafts and we sat making notes together. Then when I was in Sweden directing Beckett, I was at the Royal Dramatic Theatre, which of course is where Strindberg was based. So I was able to talk to lots of academics and dramaturgs there, to learn what was obscure because we don't know about Swedish history, and what was obscure because it was just obscure. All of that was fed back to Caryl.

Do they feel there are obscurities that are artistic flaws rather than just inaccuracies?

They're quite reverent about it in a way. There are things that a nineteenth-century audience would understand, but which for us seem weird. There are things that Swedish people today would understand, but in Britain we would find weird, for example, the pasting of the cracks in the window. In Sweden nowadays they have double windows, like they have in a lot of Europe. We don't have that: double glazing came in the 1960s and 1970s. They used to get strips of wallpaper and stick them round the windows to stop the cold air coming in. That's very much of that time and that country, but it's very opaque for us.

What do you think the play says about humanity, and why does it resonate today?

The changes we've made are attempts to make it relevant. I think in its own right, before we interfered with it, it was relevant formally more than in terms of its ideas structure, which is quite thin and clunky. Relationships don't work, there's a bit about war, there's some token left-wing politics, the big idea in it is loneliness, but it's not got a particularly strong ideas structure.

But as a formal experiment done in 1901 without any knowledge of Freud's book *The Interpretation of Dreams*, it's unbelievably radical and extraordinary. It was the first attempt to do a surrealistic play, to do a dream on stage, and even now, over a hundred years later, there are things we as theatre makers can learn from it formally. When you represent human experience on stage, you don't have to do it with plodding linear narrative or realism, there are many other choices. Nowadays there's a lot of caution about form, so I think the play is absolutely relevant from that point of view.

I think the subject matter of dreams also makes it relevant. People are looking to have how they experience things represented differently. We've all had anxiety dreams, about our teeth falling out, or about ageing, or where we can't reach a loved one, or we're back in school and being asked to do our times table. Strindberg has really put his finger on those private anxieties we all have: they're tiny details, but they're huge in a dream landscape, and that really speaks to people.

We've added a lot more dreams. We've read Freud's book and some Jung, and used some of their dreams and also our own. Because we couldn't work out how to move from one scene to another without using very clichéd conventions or awful scene changes, we had to insert dream material to get us from one scene to the next, and that then took on a life of its own. There are also fragments of improvisation, mainly in the transitional places, but sometimes in the scenes themselves.

Aside from the dreams, what kind of research did you do, or ask the actors to do?

Quite a few of the actors read Strindberg's biography. I looked back at what was happening in his own life at the time he wrote the play. All those meetings in Stockholm were about very specific details – what does it mean when he says chrysanthemum or hollyhock – is there any significance? We went through it with a fine-tooth comb, to check the meaning. We did some research into the Eastern religion he was drawing on and found he hadn't researched it well.

How did you make the decision about the dreamer?

We spent the first two weeks of rehearsal analysing dreams and reading the text. We started staging dreams, looking at the kind of dreams that work. We couldn't fly the actors, because we didn't have the budget for harnesses. We looked at the components of dreams, what makes that a dream and that not a dream, and what conventions we needed to convince the audience that they're watching a dream. Then it became really clear that we had to make a decision that one person was dreaming.

We thought there were three candidates: the Banker (whom we had made a Broker and in Strindberg's version was an Officer), Agnes and the Writer. We thought the Writer was a bit thin, there's not much about him, he comes in later and he's slightly functional, if not gnomic. Agnes has no back history at all. The only person who had one, and one that chimed with the events of Strindberg's life, was the Broker. A lot of autobiographical information was coming through, for example about the early death of his mother, or descriptions of certain visits involving foxgloves and bees, which had either happened in Strindberg's life, or gave the impression they had.

Once we had decided to set it in 1950 and in London, we built a very detailed biography of Alfred Greene the Broker, taking evidence from the play, putting the events – including two world wars – in as markers. For example, the mother says in the play, 'I was a maid once, or have you forgotten?' So we thought, she has to be a maid, so when does she become a maid and how did the maid marry someone who clearly wasn't of that class? And where did that lead us? We looked at Strindberg's biography because his mother was a maid, and we studied the history of maids in Britain, and pieced it all together. Also, every character who occurs in the dream exists in the waking world, or is a faceless person, as you often get in dreams. For example, we decided the Broker would put his first wife as the stage-door keeper. Having studied the logic of dreams, we realised that sometimes you beam down the weirdest people into different roles or jobs.

So it was a skeleton from the text, which we fleshed out with our own invention. We improvised lots of the Broker's back history, and decided that Agnes was his secretary and that he knew nothing about her – which is often the case, you often know nothing about the history of the people you work most closely with. So he dreams of his secretary Agnes Bruce as an angel coming to rescue him. This leaves some of the text behind and draws other ideas forward. In rehearsal it's been a huge evolution – so much so that we had to write a very careful note in the programme, which made it clear that what people were seeing wasn't totally Strindberg's original text or totally Caryl's version, but that there were more steps in between.

How have you worked with Vicki Mortimer, the designer?

We were in Stockholm together doing the Beckett play, so she was part of the process of historical research and research into Strindberg's life. We realised that most dreams happen in real places, in a kitchen or a location that you know, but things happen in it that don't normally happen there. So we decided we would have to have an environment that would be very real, but that could also change from one place to another, using lights and a moving wall – there are forty scenes and thirty quick changes. So we have a composite room, inspired by photos of a lovely decayed old industrial building, Ellis Island, the old customs house for New York City, before they did it up in the late 1980s. Because there's a quarantine scene in the play we rather liked that synchronicity. The setting is one we could change from a small domestic space to a large public one by moving a wall down and up. But it's also a very real one.

Has Caryl been sitting in on rehearsals and feeding her thoughts to you?

Yes, and it's been fantastic to have her involved. The deal was that she would do the version but have no obligation beyond that. But she has come in quite a lot, and she has given us really precise and useful notes. Of course, it's hard for her to see some of the text that she wrote for us being cut, or else manipulated in a different way. But they're a terribly inventive group of actors and what they're adding to the material is very stimulating. So she's very seduced by that, while also wanting to honour Strindberg. I think it's a difficult position at times, but she's such a wise woman, she can see why we're doing this, and that there would be no point in trying to yank it back in the other direction.

Has she had to add any material?

A lot of the dream text she loves and doesn't want to alter. But when we try to improvise things she always helps us out. She'll say, 'That line's at the end of the scene, so I think you should change it,' or, 'I don't think that quite works,' or, 'If you're going to do that, then I think you should do this.' She has laser-like precision in helping us with the detail.

Very strange territory

Angus Wright found himself unexpectedly cast in the lead role in *A Dream Play*

What was your first response on reading Caryl Churchill's version?
When Katie sent it to me she gave me instructions not to read any other version. I think she was worried, rightly so, that the actors would look at earlier versions and wonder what was going on. But Caryl has made it poetic and modern, and I think it speaks much more directly to us. Going from her version to our final one was a process that most other leading playwrights would have felt battered by. She wasn't, and that was amazing. I suppose it's partly the kind of tradition she's worked in, for example with Joint Stock. She understands the process the whole team needs to go through to get the result, rather than just saying, 'This is what I've written, so you either do it as it is, or not at all.'

What made you decide to accept the part?
I wanted to do it because I know Katie's work: I had been part of her company for *Three Sisters*. That was really the driving force for me. I put myself into the position of the director and I thought, 'I wouldn't know where to take the first step with this play.' But I was confident that Katie wouldn't be doing it if she didn't have some concept of where it might go. Also, we had done a workshop on brain science, where we had discussed how emotions are physical. For example, if a bear walks round the corner you don't think, 'Oh, I'm frightened.' Your body reacts, the emotion hits you and it's a physical reaction, and only afterwards do you monitor what happened and put a name to the emotion: fear.

To perform this production you need to be in tune with primary emotions like fear and disgust, anger, happiness and sadness. You mustn't censor, as we often do as actors. When you watch someone genuinely react to something with a primary emotion it can be startling and quite ugly, and it makes you think, 'Do I really do that?' So we were tapping into that area, and I knew that Katie was going to fold that work in, and the idea of dreams, and how the brain functions in dreams. I also knew that Caryl's material would be fertile territory for finding out how to make it work. It's a play that has a history of directors pitting their wits against it, and that's an interesting challenge for a company.

Presumably you had no idea before rehearsals began that you would become the central figure who has the dream?

No. Katie talked to me about playing the Banker, who is the Officer in Strindberg's play. In the early weeks of rehearsal, when we were trying to find out how to present it, he became the Broker. It's a great part to play, but it is entirely dependent on the other actors who create the dream world around the Broker. All of us are operating in very strange territory, because you reach a point where you go, 'Yes, I suppose I can do that, I can wear that, I can sing that, why not? It's a dream.' We also came up with this phrase 'faceless person', a figure who is threatening for us as human beings: the blank expression of people under umbrellas, or of those who come into a space and just look at you. All in all it's a very strange world to be working in.

Did you contribute particular dreams yourself?

There are a few of mine in there, but I'm one of those people who rarely remembers their dreams. The 'compound eyes of the bee' was mine. There are some of Freud's, some of Jung's, but most of them are ours and Katie's – and Nick Hytner has one in there too. Interestingly, since we've been on stage I've started to dream more vividly, though I don't know whether that's something I do anyway when a play is up and running.

So in rehearsal you were analysing dreams and then improvising from them?

That was fascinating. One of the things that Katie does is to use the Stanislavsky technique of working on the back history of characters. It was part of the process to flesh out people like Alfred. He doesn't exist as Alfred Greene in the original play, or in Caryl's version, so through improvisations we built up his history, the childhood home that he grew up in, his brother George, what the relationship with his parents was – everyone who was part of his family, we charted their lives. It was like a jigsaw puzzle or a detective story, trying to work out what had happened.

What do you find most helpful in the way Katie works as a director?
She's brilliant at getting inside your head, so that she knows, sometimes even before you do, what it is that is distracting you from achieving clarity. She can tell if there's interference, and even if she can't nail what that interference is, she knows it's there. She'll say, 'Your intention is to get your father to ask for forgiveness and you seem to be off that intention.' And even if the actor says, 'It's because my foot was trapped under the leg of the table,' she'll say, 'Right, we need to solve that.' It's rare that a director can have that sort of precision and care, and get right in there behind the actors' eyes. People who work with her appreciate that. It is demanding of everyone around her, to come up to that standard. But then why bother to do the work if you don't want to set the bar higher?

You had longer to rehearse than usual. Why was that?
If you do improvisational background work and the text isn't finalised, you need those extra weeks. If the play is done and dusted, and the text is fixed, then you don't need as long. We'd never worked together as a group and that chemistry, especially in a show like this, takes a little time to get right. As well as the acting, the demands of the production – which is physical and balletic and choreographed – require incredible collaboration. For example, you have to make sure that as you move that bed you're not running over someone's foot, or crashing into the stage crew backstage. Your awareness of everyone on stage needs to be acute. And the confined space, and the nature of the work, mean that backstage is just madness – it's rather like *Noises Off*. It's incredibly intense for everyone – dressers, stage management, crew, actors.

174

An enormous amount of your part involves just reacting to what is going on around you. Is that difficult?

It's true, my time on stage is peppered with my reactions to things, and there were moments in rehearsal when I thought, 'Surely I can't be surprised again, can I?' But we dealt with it by always discussing the different moments: what is the nature of this threat, or of someone's appearance, or why is the TV frightening, is it maybe a recurring dream? We decided some of this stuff on the hoof. Basically it was finding levels of unease or outright terror, and grading your reactions to the various things that happened.

How have you coped with the huge physical demands of the production?

We did ballet work and ballroom dancing right through rehearsals. Kate Flatt, who is a trained ballet dancer, choreographed a routine for us, a set of exercises, which we now do before the show. We've all got fit through doing this production, because it is non-stop – it's a bit like middle-distance running. Seeing us all in tutus is alone worth the price of admission! Getting it all to happen technically was the big battle. The more technical work you do, the further you are from the improvisational work you did in rehearsals and the delicate world you built up then. It's very hard to concentrate on getting the technical stuff right, and then in previews having to reinvest in the life of the character that you've built up.

How have audiences reacted to the first dozen or so performances?

I'm sure there are some people who are looking for narrative structure and are frustrated that they're not being given that. But it is called *A Dream Play*, so there's a hint in there that it's not going to be a whodunnit. We're getting some laughter, but that's not always a good barometer, and it can also make you start to become too aware of the audience. One of Katie's expressions is 'turning the volume down on the audience'. It's hard to blot out that world and concentrate on the one you're inhabiting on stage.

It's rare when you start rehearsals that you don't have some image of what a production will be like, that you can't picture how it will be in front of an audience. With this one I don't think any of us had any idea where we were heading, and that was very exciting. I love doing it. It has so many different settings and moods – you're caught up in a storm, then you're at your own strangely peaceful funeral, and then you're a child playing musical chairs. There's a great range that we can all play in and it has all the colours in the palette.

A Dream Play opened in the Cottesloe in February 2005.

Breaking down the fourth wall

Anthony Clark is directing a mobile production of Brecht's *Mother Courage and Her Children*

Mother Courage's washing line is causing a bit of a problem. 'That's a funny way to hang a sheet,' says the director. 'My daughter's a funny girl,' retorts Mother Courage. It's a characteristic bit of rehearsal repartee in a production of *Mother Courage and Her Children* that's trying to get away from an over-reverential approach to Brecht's classic play. 'It doesn't have to be a dirge,' Anthony Clark says. 'It's surprising how much humour we've found in it.'

In a spacious room in Lambeth, the company for the latest mobile production is in the fourth week of rehearsal. The striking but simple set, designed to fit different spaces on tour, is in place, dominated by the famous wagon, hung with the assorted belts, boots, boxes and utensils on which Mother Courage's livelihood depends. Clark has opted for a mid-twentieth-century setting and costumes, with a 1940s radio set on stage. But that was not the original choice. 'At first, with Bosnia in mind, we wondered whether to mix modern with period references,' he recalls. 'But we decided it would be patronising to people going through the war, as if you could explain it by doing *Mother Courage*.'

The company is using a version of the text by Hanif Kureishi, which aims to make the language more modern and accessible. The actors have been cast partly for the variety of accents they can offer: scouse, Welsh, south London. 'Brecht's characters work on the land, but we didn't want to end up with a generalised Mummerset sound,' Clark says. The music is also different. During the rehearsal Saira Todd, who plays Yvette, sings a haunting unaccompanied version of 'The Fraternisation Song' – not the familiar Paul Dessau version, but a new one written by composer Mark Vibrans, who has provided fresh music for all the songs.

Despite these changes, Clark has tried to respect Brecht's belief that the audience should not become passive spectators of the play. He's done this by using certain techniques that engage them in the action. 'Brecht wanted to celebrate the theatricality of his stories, so we're trying to break down the fourth wall,' he says. That theatricality becomes evident towards the end of the rehearsal, when Ellie Haddington as Courage and Jeremy Swift as the Cook work on the 'Solomon Song' with movement coach Pat Garrett. With Vibrans at the piano, they devise a humorous sequence that would have knocked 'em in the Old Kent Road.

Mother Courage doing a music-hall routine is certainly light years away from the solemnity of the Berliner Ensemble. But how will audiences react? 'Brecht didn't want her to be seen as a heroine,' Clark says. 'But when you watch somebody going through what she does, you do start to think of her as a victim of circumstances, even though she has choices.'

Mother Courage and Her Children toured in 1993, opening in the Cottesloe in December.

Having fun with Brecht

Diana Rigg has no intention of playing Mother Courage as a drudge

Two years ago, in the mobile touring production of *Mother Courage and Her Children*, we had the East End version of

Brecht's indomitable survivor. Now it's the Yorkshire version that's come to the National, courtesy of Diana Rigg.

'I decided to play her northern because I come from the north and she's got all those northern qualities,' the actress said, during a break in rehearsals in the National. 'She has this rough humour, a stubborn refusal to accept defeat, and a habit of talking about people as if they're not there – all very northern.'

It was Jonathan Kent's idea to commission a new adaptation of the play from David Hare, after the two had collaborated in similar fashion last year on Brecht's *The Life of Galileo*. But Diana Rigg is clearly in sympathy with their aim of blowing the cobwebs off this particular classic. 'Because it's about a woman pulling a cart round the stage for three and a half hours, everybody assumes that it's a mega-glum play. Yet Brecht himself kept on saying that you should have fun in rehearsals – though with some of the adaptations you read, I don't see how you could.'

David Hare's version is different, she says. 'There's a hell of a lot of handed-down tradition about Brecht, not all of it spot on, not necessarily what he wanted. What David has done is remarkable: he's kept the play as it is, but made it alive and fresh and accessible and real and *funny*.' She believes Brecht has a lot of jokes, but that they usually get lost in translation. 'Also people stood in such awe of him, they didn't associate him with humour, which was wrong. The same happens with Chekhov: his plays have this aura around them of classics in another language. As a result they can seem fusty and dusty, so that it's like watching marionettes rather than real people.'

Brecht once said that Mother Courage shouldn't be thought of as a heroine. But don't modern audiences sympathise with her plight? 'I can't begin to concern myself with that, I just play her,' Rigg says. 'The one thing that Brecht didn't want is for you to be remotely sentimental at any point, and I hope I shall be vigilant in not being so. Anyway, I hate it when actors play for sympathy.'

If she's sticking to the alienation principle, she's planning to break another tradition. 'Most people play Mother Courage like an old drudge,' she says. 'Now I certainly won't be the most glamorous of women on stage, but I see no reason to look like a bag lady. On the contrary, I shall be quite gaily dressed.' She cites plenty of evidence in the text for this sprucing-up of the character's image. 'She's been around, has Mother Courage: she's got three children by three different husbands and sex is not something unknown to her. Nor, for that matter, is she past it now, otherwise the Cook and the Chaplain wouldn't like being around her so much.'

Having played other meaty parts such as Cleopatra, Hedda Gabler and Medea, what particular qualities does she need for Mother Courage? 'Stamina,' she says instantly. 'She's like a steamroller through the play, she's just inexorable. Even at the end, when her daughter has died, she gets up and starts pushing that cart again.'

Mother Courage and Her Children opened in the Olivier in November 1995.

Reviving Brecht

Howard Davies and Sean Holmes explain why the creator of epic theatre is still important

Productions of Brecht's plays have been a little thin on the ground recently. Now, courtesy of the National, along come two, one close behind the other: an 'intimate version' by David Hare of *The Life of Galileo*, to be staged in the Olivier by Howard Davies, and *The Caucasian Chalk Circle*, directed by Sean Holmes as a mobile production, using Frank McGuinness' version.

'Brecht is one of the great dramaturgical geniuses of the twentieth century,' Howard Davies says. 'We've been hugely influenced by his theories and his practice, by his plays and his poetry. But sometimes people have been too reverential and have ended up doing dour productions, with no set and no costumes and absolutely no life. Unfortunately he got appropriated by the Left, who turned his plays into blackboard-and-chalk public lectures. Actually, he's the reverse of all that: what he was saying was that you can make theatre vibrant with very little. His plays have tremendous theatrical brio.'

Sean Holmes, too, is critical of the way the plays have often been staged. 'Ten years ago there was a rush of productions, which either slavishly followed the theory, or went completely the other way,' he says. 'They made Brecht seem dusty, when in fact he is quite the opposite. In responding to the well-made play he was influenced by the Greeks and Shakespeare and the Jacobeans, but he used them in a very modern way. His writings can also surprise you, when you find him, for example, talking about good theatre being "instructive fun".'

Both directors are in no doubt of the relevance of Brecht's plays for today. 'With *Galileo* you suddenly become aware how pertinent some of the arguments are,' Davies observes. 'For example, the one between the emerging culture of science and the established culture of religion. The play is also about – not exactly freedom of speech, but the freedom to pursue certain ideas. Brecht rewrote it after Hiroshima, when scientists realised for the first time that there might be a limit to how far you should pursue the scientific quest. That idea went into the new version.'

The Caucasian Chalk Circle may be set in Azerbaijan in 'olden times', but it too has a modern political resonance. 'I think there's a danger that every play you do ends up being about Iraq,' Holmes warns. 'I certainly don't intend to make any overt connection, but you can obviously see a modern parallel, in that the play deals partly with a state in chaos. But the primary reason for doing it is that it's a good play: whether you're fourteen or a hundred and four, you can respond to it.'

His version, involving nine actors and musicians, is likely to be unusually vibrant, since it's a co-production with the inventive devising company Filter. Founded in 2001 by actors Oliver Dimsdale and Ferdy Roberts and musician Tim Phillips, Filter create a bold fusion on stage of live and recorded music, naturalistic and stylised physical movement, and video images. 'Brecht favoured slides, but if this kind of technology had been around then, I think he would have used it,' Holmes says. 'Filter work in a way that exposes the process, which fits with Brecht's intentions. It seemed like perfect synergy, to use their creativity and freedom.'

For Davies *The Life of Galileo* has an epic subject matter but a style that is intimate, which makes it a challenge to get the staging right in the large spaces of the Olivier. He's likely to drop the banner descriptions that precede each scene in the text. 'To go back to a technique that poked the audience in the eye seems very old hat,' he suggests. He also plans to restore the famous carnival scene to how Brecht wrote it; in Hare's version, written in 1994, the street players have become puppets. 'I think you lose the contrast with the scene at the ball if you don't use the players as representatives of the common people.'

He acknowledges his good fortune in being able to cast Simon Russell Beale as Galileo. 'He's a brilliant actor, with this phenomenal gift for language. In a piece like this, dealing with cosmology and science and philosophy, to have someone of Simon's talent and intelligence is just fabulous.'

The Life of Galileo opened in the Olivier in June 2006. *The Caucasian Chalk Circle* began touring in January 2007.

MODERN AMERICAN DRAMA

Eagerly seeking Sophie

Fiona Shaw and Stephen Daldry explore
Machinal, a classic play by a neglected
American feminist

'I'm always in pursuit of big plays, so it was very thrilling to
find this one, because it feels like a giant classic.' Fiona Shaw
has played her fair share of meaty parts from the classical
repertoire. In the last three years alone she's given powerful
performances in the title roles in *Hedda Gabler, The Good
Person of Sichuan* and *Electra.* Yet the part of the heroine in
Machinal is, she believes, as challenging as any of these.

   Machinal (in French 'mechanical' or 'automatic') is the
moving story of a young woman trapped in a mechanistic
urban world. Eventually caught up in a suffocating marriage,
she's driven to murder her insensitive husband and goes to the
electric chair for her crime. 'It's a wonderful play, like a Greek
tragedy, and I'm sometimes overwhelmed by its size and
sadness,' Shaw says, during a break in rehearsals. 'It's a
revolutionary work, and not one that reveals itself easily. So
you have to dig like mad to get at the subtext, and be very true
to what you find coming out.'

   Based on the real-life murder case of Ruth Snyder, a
housewife who killed her husband in the 1920s, it was written
by Sophie Treadwell, an American playwright and journalist
who sat in on the celebrated murder trial. It was first produced
in New York in 1928 (Clark Gable played the young lover),
since when it has rarely been performed. In form the play is
expressionist, though its author never used such a label. It
mixes naturalistic scenes with others that attempt to catch the

bleak, jerky rhythms of city life, in a style foreshadowing Beckett, Pinter and Mamet. Treadwell also punctuates the story with several extraordinary stream-of-consciousness monologues that chart the inner workings of the heroine's anguished mind and soul.

It was partly this originality of form that made director Stephen Daldry want to do the play. 'It's a feminist play that belongs to a lost tradition of women's theatre work, which is rarely celebrated,' he says. 'Other women were writing at the time in America, but their work was not challenging stylistically. Sophie Treadwell tried to reinvent the form, and came up with this deft marriage of style and content.' But he was also attracted to the play for the moral issues it raises, such as whether a woman can ever be justified in killing her husband. 'It's a pretty fundamental attack on the institution of marriage,' he suggests. 'It also has obvious contemporary parallels with cases such as that of Sarah Thornton, and other women who have been driven to kill.'

Apart from a couple of dissertations, little has been written about Treadwell, who in addition to her thirty plays and extensive journalism also wrote novels. For Shaw this is not a problem. 'I think you learn more about people through their fiction than through fact,' she says. 'In this play you hit a very unhappy soul, who's in touch with something terribly discomforting and disquieting about the nature of relationships.' Despite the fact that she commits murder, the heroine, simply called Young Woman, is a sympathetic character, who reaches out for the ordinary things in life, but is denied them at every turn – generally by men. As Treadwell herself put it: 'She is a woman who is innately unsuited to this mechanisation of life, a woman who must love and be loved.'

The execution at the end of the play prompted Shaw to do some background reading on the subject. This included looking at an essay on Gary Gilmour by his brother, at Turgenev's account of an execution in 1870, and at the story of the notorious trial of the Rosenbergs in 1953. 'I was interested in the seeming ordinariness of the people who were executed,' she says. 'They're stories of moments when time slows down, moments of seeming nobility when people transcend themselves, even though they're alone, and no matter what their crime is.'

Rehearsals for the play are demanding. 'Plays are about travelling in an inner landscape, they give you a chance to really forage,' Shaw suggests. 'But it's important to be with fellow foragers. It is marvellous working with Stephen, because he sits on his donkey and rides well into the unknown. But you have to be brave, not disconcerted, and go that league further. You have to throw out good ideas and remain muddled for much longer.'

For Daldry the big question is whether an experimental play such as *Machinal* can work in the Lyttelton, whether its themes are big enough for such a theatre. Coping with the mixed style of the play is also a challenge. 'Fiona is a wonderfully open actress, and we are throwing it up in the air and seeing how it comes down,' he says. 'But style is very difficult to impose, because a play dictates its own style, and you have to respond to what emerges.'

Machinal opened in the Lyttelton in October 1993.

The great experimenter

Howard Davies on directing Eugene O'Neill's *Mourning Becomes Electra*

What were the play's particular challenges for you?
The melodramatic form which O'Neill deploys made it a very tricky work to stage. It's been a real balancing act between playing things truthfully and observing his high-octane, red-blood-cell take on all these characters. Their mendacity, that they can say one thing and then go out and promptly do another, is there for all to see, and that's wonderful; we all love watching people behaving badly. But there are times when he just uses the device once too often. So I've cut nearly six hundred lines – which is why our production runs at four

hours twenty minutes rather than the original six and a half hours.

O'Neill is a devil to direct because he goes on these mind-bending experimental journeys. With *The Hairy Ape*, for example, he's emulating European expressionism; then he sets about writing *Mourning Becomes Electra* in the form of a Greek tragedy. In his diary writings about the play, he says he wants to write something that is realistic, yet he also wants to use the Greek form. He wrestles with this continually, he beats himself over the head with it.

Did he seriously consider having the actors in masks?

At one point he did. He starts a draft and says, I have to get rid of the masks and the big soliloquies directed to the audience, and he finds that this is much better. He then tries for a second time to put the masks and soliloquies in and, when that fails, he abandons the idea. So it takes him nearly a year to write the play, having tried various styles. Later in some other note he says he would prefer to have future productions done in masks – but he's wrong!

Did you make small cuts throughout, rather than cut any major part of a scene?

Yes. Our designer Bob Crowley was always urging me to cut the short introductory townsfolk scenes, but I felt you had to keep them in. Of course there's a fat chance of them being seen as a Greek chorus, as O'Neill wanted. But what they do is socialise the play in some way. Bob felt the scenes were unworkable, clunky, badly written, simplistic – and to a certain extent he's right. But they're not without life or humour, and if you get a sufficiently committed group of actors you can make them work.

Why did you have a read-through before you finally cast the production?

It was in order to persuade Helen Mirren to do the play. She kept on reading it to herself and saying, 'I don't get this.' So we sat down for three days and, after working on certain scenes, at the end she was able to say, 'Oh I get it, I see it.' It was not that she wasn't capable of it, there's no disregard of Helen. Quite understandably – as did most of the people when I first talked to them about being in the production – she saw it as quite operatic in its form and very overblown.

Part of my persuading Helen was saying, 'Please don't read those lengthy stage directions.' At the end of three days she said, 'I begin to see how it works.' I said, 'Yes, in an actor's mouth, in yours and everyone else's around this table, it's working because you're not responding to his directions; he's not written lines that are inflated and crazy, but he's written directions which are.' I was so fed up with having meetings with actors who said 'I don't get it' that we cut all the stage directions, and they just had the lines. So we approached rehearsals as if it were a new play. At the first reading everyone went, 'Oh God, this is so much easier than I thought.'

Did you do the same when you directed The Iceman Cometh?

No, because it's written ten years later and O'Neill has gone back to a form that is less experimental. With *Mourning Becomes Electra* he's really pushing the boat out, and in the end he finds that he can't, and he comes back to something he was always banging on about in his notes, of creating something psychologically real. But he's also tormenting himself by saying, 'How can I write a tragedy in a Greek style in a world that no longer believes in either fate or God?' So he knows he's setting himself a problem.

But with *The Iceman Cometh* they're a set of recognisable characters he remembers from his youth, from the time he bummed around, and nearly became an alcoholic and tried to commit suicide. These are based on real people, they're not mythic fictional characters. He's writing language as he remembers it. He does overwrite the characterisation and you have to deal with that, but they're much more recognisable.

Was one part of the trilogy more difficult to work on than the others?

All the critics say Play 3 is the least well written. I don't think it is. What they've missed is that O'Neill cheats and writes it in a different style. Greek drama is like soap opera: it's not a question of *what's* going to happen, it's *how* it's going to happen. You watch with a kind of delight that you're in advance of the characters. And there's something very soap opera about *Mourning Becomes Electra*: you usually know what's going to happen, so you get a salacious thrill. But in Play 3 you haven't got a clue what's going to happen. Just as you're wondering what else O'Neill can say, he abandons the Greek storyline and writes something new.

In Play 3 he's writing about guilt. Orin and Lavinia are destroying each other not because they don't like each other, as happens with the characters in the first two plays. On the contrary, they love each other as brother and sister, and they're inextricably bound up because they've been abused in one way or another by one of their parents, and have then gone on this journey of revenge. But Orin is being used as a tool by the sister, and therefore finds himself in a state of incredible guilt and will not let her go or escape unpunished. They drag each other down into this whirlpool. In that sense it's inexorable, but I don't think you spot what's going to come.

Did you give the actors any guidance about style before you started rehearsing?

I was being a bit faux-naïve and disingenuous, because I said at the beginning, I'm not sure if this play throws up problems of style, I think these characters have to be real, but the scale of the events – two murders, two suicides and a bout of incest – is a little bit big. The only way to approach it is by making the characters recognisable if not realistic: the audience are not going to sit there for that length of time unless they can say, 'Oh I see why she's done that.' It's not opera, you can't just sing your way through it, you have to allow the audience to spot *why* things are happening – why he is so jealous, why she's annoying him and so on. Therefore it has to be as real as possible. The tricky thing is that, given that brief, the actors' instinct is to play everything very detailed and low key. So you just have to slowly open it up. It's like becoming an athlete, you just slowly develop and develop your muscle, to allow you to be real, but still to play it very strongly.

Has playing to the preview audiences forced you to make any significant changes?

We have to be careful, because the British ironic take is different from the full-on American way of doing things. Some of the younger members of the audience, on certain nights, found some of the moments risible, and we've had to work out how to get round that.

Were these the extreme moments?

No, funnily enough they were the throwaway moments, moments that followed extreme violence. For example, after Orin tells Christine he's killed Brant, she starts moaning, and he says in an offhand way, 'Mother, don't moan like that.' And they laughed. So we now play it harsher. If you take the pressure off, people laugh; but if he really goes for her, then you feel for her because he's being so violent, you feel he should allow her to have her grief. So if you play it selfishly and cruelly, then the audience aren't going to laugh; play it offhand and they will.

Bob Crowley's set is truly amazing: were you happy with it from the start?

When we first started talking about it, Bob showed me a photograph of a house that he'd put a cross against in a book of his. In fact it was in the South, but the architecture in the North looks very similar. It was Greek-temple, neo-classical architecture. It was an interesting photograph because it was taken within the veranda looking out, so that you were slightly involved in the house. There was an upper level, and we started trying to work out a very similar design, with an upper level and a staircase, but it got so complicated we abandoned that.

Then we had to face the problem of how to go from the outside to the inside and back again. We got ourselves very tangled up in the Rubik Cube of trying to make that work. Bob solved it by splitting the wall, allowing various shapes to emerge. It became slightly unrealistic, but I embraced that, because I realised that if we started breaking the rooms up as the play becomes more nightmarish, that would be fine.

There was also the problem of the ship. O'Neill doesn't give you an interval either side of it, you have to go straight to it and then back again. One day Bob and I were looking at early cardboard models of the set, and looking at the pillars, and we both said, 'I suppose we could use the pillars for the masts.' That conversation gave him the idea of using the ceiling and tipping it. I said, 'We'll never get away with that, because it will involve torque' – the way he wanted it to tip meant that it would have to tip down at an angle. Having gone to the engineers, who said it was impossible, he managed to work it out by building the ceiling as a three-dimensional piece – it looks as if it's lowering and twisting, but it's not. It was a wonderful solution.

How much did you talk about the music to your composer Dominic Muldowney?

He came to see a run-through and afterwards he said, 'The only purposive music I can do is similar to what Bob is doing with the set, which is to move the play forward. I have to shunt it into the next scene, but not comment on the scene, it's got to be a different voice altogether. It's not like picking up Christine's voice, it's just got to go, "This is big, and this is moving forwards."' I said I thought that sounded rather ruthless, so he suggested he put together some pieces. I listened to them and realised he was right.

It's very subtle, the way he works in tunes such as the 'Battle Hymn' and 'Shenandoah'.

Yes, it's almost subliminal. At the beginning it sets up a whole landscape, which suggests something spooky, something slightly epic. You can hear the battle in the background, a bit of fife and drum. But it's done as a memory, it's a collage of sound that refers back to the civil war that's ending. All his music is linked to scene changes, apart from one moment when Lavinia dances for Peter. That's an invention, it's not in the script, I just thought she should do it, we should see a difference in her. We're approaching Play 3 with a woman who started as a young, studious, slightly prickly intellectual, deeply resentful of her mother's infidelity and sexual waywardness. Then she grows into a fully sexualised being. I wanted to express that with a little underscoring at that moment.

I'm extremely lucky to have an artistic team that has in it people like Dominic and Bob, and Mark Henderson who does the lighting. I can express my passion for certain aspects of what they're doing and my dislike of other aspects, and nobody takes offence, because we're all working towards the same goal.

Keeping the lid on

Tim Pigott-Smith on being Ezra Mannon

Were you already familiar with Mourning Becomes Electra?
Yes, I came across it when I was studying drama at Bristol
University. I was completely hooked, and for the next three
weeks I did nothing but read all his other plays. What I liked
about them was not just their emotional power, which could
make you laugh and cry, but also their sheer size and scope.
Does that emotional power create problems for a modern actor?
It does, because however you look at *Mourning Becomes Electra*,
it's a melodrama and you're dealing with extremes. This makes
it difficult to get the level of intensity right, so in rehearsals with
Howard it's been a matter of seeing how far you can go before
you introduce a false note, then bringing the whole thing back
– keeping the lid on, as he keeps telling us.
What about O'Neill's stage directions and character descriptions?
They're insanely detailed. When we did *The Iceman Cometh* we
found them very restrictive, as we did those wretched brackets
that say 'intensely' or 'passionately' or 'sardonically'. With
Mourning Becomes Electra we used the full script for the read-
through, and Helen said how limiting she found them. So
Howard had the script printed out without them, without even
exits and entrances – and it cut the length by some fifty pages.
It's remarkable how much that freed up the imagination. Since
then I haven't felt the need to go back to the stage directions.
We're being very honourable to the script, so I don't think
we're going to do anything to offend the O'Neill estate.
How did you approach your own character?
Ezra Mannon is a real puritanical, repressed New Englander. I
think it's easier to play someone who is contained than
someone who is letting it all out. In terms of modern fashion
it's much more sympathetic to suppress than release, at least in
England. What's difficult about Ezra is to find out *how* he lets
it out, and *why*. Before his first entrance we've heard so much
about him being uptight, yet he comes on and after a very short
time spills his guts out to his wife. You've got about twenty

lines to establish the man and then you go against character, which is peculiar. But you just have to rely on the skill of the playwright. Howard doesn't direct you to play ironic, because if you comment on the play it's dead. But he allows irony to exist. The whole thing is dramatic irony – Ezra comes home and he says, 'I want to change my life, I love you' – and in the scene before Christine has organised the poison! You don't have to work at the irony, it's there, that's what the scene is.

Does the fact that it's a trilogy cause particular difficulties?

Play 3 is the hardest to make successful. The first two plays are all doing, whereas in the third the characters have to live with the consequences of what's happened. Apart from a suicide very late on, there's no strong action like in the ship scene, it's just pure gut-wrenching, screwing-people-to-the-floor, families-are-hell-and-misery stuff – which is very hard for an audience that has sat through a long evening. Also, because the play is so long, you sometimes don't rehearse a scene for ten days. So in the early stage of rehearsals a lot of the work you have done can just filter away. Helen and I went two weeks without doing one scene and when we ran through it, it was terrible. We knew it so lamentably that nothing happened at all in it.

What would you say is distinctive about Howard's style of directing?

When you start on a new play it's a nerve-racking experience, you feel vulnerable, you think you're terrible. Howard waits until you've got through that stage, then he'll give you a few notes and leave you alone again. Just when you're thinking you need to move further on, he'll throw twenty darts at you. His timing is brilliant; he understands the process of acting. He's very clear and incisive in his thinking, he knows exactly what he thinks the play is about, and he has a notion of how it should be done. But then whatever else he does he does through you. He'll only bring up those broader notions if they're relevant.

Largely speaking he doesn't work intellectually but practically. He says, 'It's good when you do that,' or, 'It's better when you do that rather than that,' or, 'I've given you a wrong note there' – so he gets people relating to each other really fast. It's a real open forum and a democratic one, he doesn't feel threatened by anyone else having ideas. The work is done in great detail, so you feel very secure, you feel impeccably rehearsed, because you know you won't say a single line about which you haven't talked at some point or another. Yet you also feel very free. It's an ideal platform – even though you feel quite raw, that's better than the opposite, the more corseted kind of direction that doesn't allow any room for error – which the audience soon smells.

Mourning Becomes Electra opened in the Lyttelton in November 2003.

Strong connections

Julie Walters has drawn on her own life to create the mother in Arthur Miller's *All My Sons*

Ten minutes ago she was Kate Keller, sobbing away on the Cottesloe stage after her husband's suicide. Now she's Julie Walters, rattling on merrily in her dressing room about motherhood, the theatre, being expelled from schools, restraining Mrs Overall, and the day she met Arthur Miller. 'It's great to be back in the theatre, I'm much more at home here,' she says. 'I suppose it's because I'm big and loud, and you have to tone everything down when you do films or television.'

All My Sons marks her first stage appearance since she played the widow in Tennessee Williams's *The Rose Tattoo* nine years ago. That was when she discovered her three-year-old daughter had leukaemia. In the intervening years she has turned down several plays, including *Six Degrees of Separation* and *The Rise and Fall of Little Voice*, in order to be with her daughter. Understandably, she connects strongly with the mother in Miller's play. 'I'm incredibly touched by the way she tries to hold on to her son,' she says. 'I remember that feeling of not being able to go forward or backwards, that paralysis. But I also love the fact that she's so strong. She has this unconditional love for her husband and she keeps it all together, which so many women do anyway.'

Her own mother was strong in a different way. 'When I told her I wanted to be an actress, she went potty. "What have we reared?" she said. "You'll be in the gutter before you're twenty." She was right, but I rather liked it.' The desire to act was there in her from an early age. 'God knows what sparked it off. I never went to the theatre, except my mother's office productions,' she says. 'But even as a child, when I watched drama on television, I used to think arrogantly, "I can do those parts, all of them – and better." It wasn't a desire to be famous or a film star, I just wanted to be on the stage.'

She was expelled from school in the sixth form. 'Not for anything appalling, I just wasn't there very much and they said I was subversive. I had to look that up in the dictionary.' Under pressure from her mother she first went into nursing. 'I quite enjoyed it in a showing-off sort of a way, doing a soft-shoe-shuffle up the ward and eating the patients' grapes, and waiting for the senior staff to go off so I could do a bit of a show.' But the acting compulsion was too strong. She applied to Manchester Polytechnic to do a course that combined acting (to please herself) and teaching (to please her mother) – though she had no intention of being a teacher. 'It felt fabulous; suddenly I was in the right gear, instead of just grinding along in second.'

Once bitten, but probably never shy, she applied to the Everyman in Liverpool to take part in their pub shows. 'I hardly knew anything about plays then,' she recalls. 'I thought Clemence Dane was a man. For my audition I rewrote some of *Juno and the Paycock*, putting some of my own jokes in without really thinking. How naïve can you get!' She started performing in some very rough pubs in Liverpool, then joined the company at the Everyman, where Willy Russell was the resident playwright. Soon after, he was commissioned by the Royal Shakespeare Company, wrote *Educating Rita* and asked Julie Walters to play Rita. The rest is herstory . . .

Howard Davies is the director of *All My Sons*. 'He's incredibly incisive,' Walters says. 'You're in your own little capsule as an actor, but he seems to be able to see it all. Although I was nervous on the first night, I've never felt so prepared in my whole life.' For a performance that *The Times* described as 'an unforgettable portrait of a maternal fixation', she has her own way of summoning up Kate Keller's anguish. 'I use an image from my childhood. I was playing with a boy in the street and when he went he left his sandwich on our wall. I remember looking at it and feeling very sad and totally alone. I key into that image before I go on.'

Although she says Mrs Overall, her celebrated television creation from *Acorn Antiques*, is in all the parts she plays ('I know she's there, she's part of my shape, I can't help it'), she tries hard to keep her away from Kate Keller. 'But I'm terrified when I come on with the tray and the headscarf. I think, "Oh God, I'd better stand up straight."' She was nervous when she heard Arthur Miller was coming to see the play. 'Usually I like knowing when people are in, but with him I didn't want to know. I was worried I'd get the lines wrong, or put in a "well" or a "but" that wasn't there. But he loved it; he cried at the end.' She sighs, remembering him with pleasure. 'He signed my copy of the play. He was lovely.'

Now she's back in the theatre she wants to do more, but has nothing lined up. The classics? 'I did Lady Macbeth in Leicester, with Nancy Meckler directing. I loved doing that.' Cleopatra then? 'Bloody hell – but perhaps I could, with the right director.' Maybe Restoration comedy? 'Helen Mirren said I should have a go at that. Something like *The Country Wife* perhaps. That would be good fun. And I wouldn't have to cry every night.'

All My Sons opened in the Cottesloe in July 2000, and transferred to the Lyttelton in August 2001.

All in the family

David Thacker, directing *Death of a Salesman*,
ponders the abiding appeal of Arthur Miller's
plays

David Thacker first became interested in Miller's plays as
artistic director of the Young Vic in the mid-1980s. 'They were
bullseye plays that fitted perfectly with our policy of attracting
young audiences,' he recalls. 'They moved and affected young
people in ways that few other plays could achieve.'

Since then he has become something of an expert in the
celebrated American playwright's work, not only directing
many of his plays (including *Broken Glass* at the National in
1994), but also working closely with Miller himself during
some of the productions. Such a collaboration took place with
Death of a Salesman, currently playing at the National. During
a World Theatre seminar in Salzburg, director and writer
worked with the four principal actors – Alun Armstrong,
Marjorie Yates, Mark Strong and Corey Johnson – on various
aspects of the play.

'If you have access to the playwright, you can have points of
interpretation confirmed or contradicted,' Thacker says. 'But
what's most useful to me is seeing Arthur push actors towards
genuinely honest and truthful performances, or challenge them
on particular lines or moments, which he feels they don't
understand.' Miller also influenced directorial decisions about
the style of the production. This moves away from a naturalistic approach, aiming to show that the memory sequences
reflect what is going through Willy Loman's mind in the
present, rather than some objectively true account of the past.
(An early title for the play was *The Inside of His Head*.)

The abiding appeal to all age groups of Miller's plays,
Thacker suggests, lies in their accessibility. He aimed to write
plays that could be understood equally well by a doctor or a
docker, plays whose story you could tell to someone on a train
and they would get it. But his work also engages audiences
because of its particular focus, because his plays often deal

with the kind of pressures that are intrinsic to family life. Willy's agonising hopes and aspirations for his eldest son Biff provide a classic example of the kind of struggle between the generations that so many people can relate to.

When the play was first performed in 1949 it was labelled 'a time bomb under capitalism'. But Thacker hasn't attempted to bring out the politics, believing them to be self-evident, and inextricably linked with the play's emotional and psychological drama. 'I don't think Miller's main concern is to show us the evils of capitalism, that's not what's bothering him,' he says. 'If you think of his plays as overtly political, you start to reduce the scale and range of what he's investigating. It's crucial to allow the complexities of the situation to be fully expressed.'

Death of a Salesman opened in the Lyttelton in October 1996.

A fascinating cocktail

Matthew Warchus on directing *Buried Child*, and the genius of his friend Sam Shepard

Sam Shepard has been called the 'bucking bronco' of American theatre. His plays have been labelled wild, unruly, surrealist, Gothic, mythic. But *Buried Child*, which captured the Pulitzer Prize in 1978, is one of his most accessible.

A powerful story of a young man returning with his girl-friend to his rural Illinois home, it draws on many of Shepard's obsessions: the search for roots, the quest for identity, the disintegrating family. 'It has so many dimensions, it feels like a classical play now,' says director Matthew Warchus, currently rehearsing the National's production. 'It's done often in the States, but it's not really known in Britain. I'm reminded of Pinter, especially a play like *The Homecoming*: you never quite know what mode you're in. There's brutality, but also playful situations: the boundaries are very fluid.'

Few directors are better qualified than Warchus to direct a Shepard play. After staging *True West* in London and New

York, he made a film of *Simpatico*, and became a close friend of the playwright – they've been to the Kentucky Derby together and he called in at Shepard's house on 9/11. 'I think it helps to know the writer,' he says. 'Working on *Buried Child* I can hear Sam's voice a lot.' He finds the plays a fascinating cocktail of elements. 'The influence of rock and roll gives his writing verve: it's intense, visceral, explosive stuff. But it also has an electrifying comic fizz and it's full of epic poetry, which is surprising.' He's using a revised version of *Buried Child*: 'The original had more ambiguities in it than Sam intended. He got fed up with seeing portentous Greek productions of the play. He wanted it to be funnier.'

In the rehearsal room the stage area is bare except for a sofa. On one wall hangs a photograph of Rob Howell's attractive set, showing a large, timber-framed room in the family home. 'It's a set that gives you a lot of scope for imaginative lighting,' Warchus says approvingly. He's equally delighted with his cast, which includes the American actors M. Emmet Walsh, veteran of 101 films, and Lauren Ambrose, who plays Claire in *Six Feet Under*. 'The grandfather is a King Lear character, so I needed an actor like Emmet, with the right vitality, authority and power. For Shelly I needed someone young but experienced: Lauren is perfect, she has the right kind of glow.'

A thoroughly modern kid

Lauren Ambrose enjoys the switch from
Six Feet Under to *Buried Child*

The young American actress knows when she's lucky. 'On *Six Feet Under* we work every day for eight months of the year. For an actor to be able to do that is rare. I feel very privileged.'

Her performance as Claire, the tough, judgemental but vulnerable daughter of the Fisher family, has been one of many pleasures in that classy, blackly comic series. But now, rehearsing for *Buried Child*, she's getting to grips with a very different role. 'Shelly is much more liquid and adaptable than

Claire: she's grown up with hippies, she's free and open, and able to talk about her emotions. It's a very interesting and exciting part.'

Red-haired and peachy skinned, with eyes wide open and an infectious giggle, she seems much younger than twenty-five. But theatrically she's no novice, having made her debut off-Broadway at fourteen. 'As a girl I studied classical voice and opera, so I was always performing,' she says. 'Then I had this acting opportunity. Working in those four-floor walk-up theatres in narrow little spaces wasn't very glamorous, but it was great playing there. I just wanted to be in that world.'

At nineteen she was briefly in London and visited the theatre every night. 'I remember watching Fiona Shaw in *The Prime of Miss Jean Brodie* from the back of the Lyttelton circle, so I have this vision of an enormous theatre with thousands of seats. Acting there will be very different from having a camera three inches from my face, talking from the back of my throat and trying to make Claire, this very modern kid, real and believable.' Happily she has an experienced director on hand. 'Matthew has incredible insights into the play, and he's so quiet and calm. I have the utmost faith in him.'

Buried Child opened in the Lyttelton in December 2004.

A dream to direct

Edward Hall on the short, sharp shock provided by David Mamet's *Edmond*

While *Edmond* has provided Kenneth Branagh with his first role at the National, it marks, too, the debut on the South Bank of director Edward Hall, who was also a stalwart of the Royal Shakespeare Company in his early days.

Usually perceived as a specialist in Shakespeare and other classic revivals, Hall has in fact directed new work at Hampstead and the Royal Court, and also tackled musicals. He's always been a huge fan of the American writer's work:

'Mamet has this fantastic ability to create big plays set in small places, such as bars or diners,' he says. 'His stories somehow assume epic proportions. I don't know of any other writer who does that today. So many plays fail because they're too small, or not theatrical enough.'

Edmond is a dark, often shocking play charting the rapid disintegration of an ordinary New Yorker after he walks out on his wife. Playing at just an hour and a quarter, with twenty-eight characters and twenty-five scenes, it's written in Mamet's characteristic style: short, sharp sentences, which conceal as much as they reveal. 'The scenes are short, but very punchy, written at just the right length to carry the story forward,' Hall says.

The play was first performed in Chicago in 1983 and in Britain two years later, with Colin Stinton in the title role in both productions. 'It's a brilliantly strong piece of drama, which feels like it was written yesterday,' Hall suggests. For the National's production Mamet provided him with a few minor updates, mostly on money matters: 'For instance, the price of sex has gone up considerably in twenty years.'

Hall sees the play as tackling two big themes of American culture. 'It deals with a classic example of a sexless white middle-class marriage, in which all the man's frustrations are channelled into activities such as sport, or going to lap-dance clubs. But it also shatters the myth that America is a multi-cultural, integrated society: it may be multicultural but it's certainly not integrated, and the play is brutally uncompromising about that.'

He says he found *Edmond* a dream to direct. 'Its language and rhythm are so beautifully crafted, you just need to let them do the work. And if you follow Mamet's ideas in his book *True or False*, it's very difficult to make a duff move.' He's also full of admiration for how boldly and speedily Kenneth Branagh worked during the three and a half weeks they spent in rehearsal.

'We talked a fair amount beforehand, but neither of us wanted to impose a complex character on the text. Once we started rehearsing he worked very fast, he just went for it. He wasn't afraid to explore the extremes, he was pushing the material to the very edge. I found him a fantastic actor to work with, and I think he illuminated the play in a very exciting way.'

A mass of contradictions

Kenneth Branagh sees Edmond as 'a kind of Everyman'

I didn't know *Edmond* before; I hadn't seen Richard Eyre's Royal Court production. So when I first read it I was very shocked by the language – not by the individual words, but the whole context of it, the savagery and brutality. In 1982 it was clearly ahead of its time, because now it feels like it was written yesterday. The urban unease it shows has caught up with us, so it seems to hold a mirror up to our times.

I think it's a moral play: it makes you think long and hard about the illusion of power. Mamet presents Edmond as a kind of Everyman, the grey man whom you ignore on the train. He reflects the mass of seething contradictions in all of us. He flirts with racism and homophobia, but finds these are not the answers. He rebels against a lack of civilised living, but the terrible price he pays shows you can't do that with violence. Mamet points you in the direction of tolerance, he suggests that Edmond's journey is not one to follow. I think there is some source of hope in it.

It's powerful and intelligent writing that as an actor you want to serve. Edward Hall says it's like *Hamlet* or *Richard III* squashed into a very small box. But although the play only lasts seventy-five minutes, I never get to the bottom of the part. It's so compelling, there's a huge amount to discover, you could play it for a very long time and still find new things, which is the stimulus you need for a long run.

The text is like a score, a musical orchestration: every pause is marked, every emphasis is in italics, so it's important to stick to Mamet's instructions. If you do an extra pause, to try to show you're suffering, it just doesn't work. Playing it requires absolute precision, you can't be fluffy; and if ever speech needed to be spoken trippingly on the tongue, this is it. There's no pressure to do in-depth characterisation. When I met Mamet I said, 'You've given this man a name, an address and a job. Is there a particular New York voice you want?' 'No,' he said, 'he's undistinguished, he's neutral.' He didn't want the actor to bring in any more detail, any character tics or inner exploration, any life history. In that sense his work is like Shakespeare's: the words *are* the characters.

Edmond was previously seen as minor Mamet and produced in a chamber fashion, with just six or seven actors doubling up. Ed wanted to try it with a large cast in a big space, so the epic dimension could emerge. I think he's been very faithful to Mamet's intentions. He has a great respect for the writing. He's a rigorous director and a worrier, in a positive way. He's good at offering little brushstrokes, especially at the beginning and end of scenes, so the audience doesn't have time to settle.

The audiences have surprised us. The play has provoked more varied reactions than any other show I've been in. We've had all kinds of laughter, comfortable and uncomfortable, and even the odd seat going up – some people are shocked by the visceral emotions. They don't have time for a considered reaction, they respond instinctively. And what we hear is that they've been disturbed. It's a very good example of live theatre: it's not indulgent, it unsettles you.

The audiences make a huge contribution, they complete the circle. On stage you have to be prepared for anything. You go on with your intentions, but you find the way you say the lines changes every night. The pin-drop silence in the pauses, the concentration, are a great tribute to Mamet's writing. For me, it's been almost like learning to act again.

Edmond opened in the Olivier in July 2003.

MODERN ENGLISH AND IRISH DRAMA

Not moving, but hoping

Fiona Shaw is up to her neck in Beckett's *Happy Days*

What is the special appeal to you of Beckett's work?
When I did his play *Footfalls* there was a fantastic voice in it, unlike anything else I've ever done. Those marvellous jumps in and out of reality make you realise he is an absolute master of the theatre. One is always looking for writers who are not revealing but hiding, and he really understood the essence of burying extraordinary things in ordinary meaning. He's not gloomy, he's very funny. He does what all great artists do, he reminds you what it is to be human.

Winnie spends most of the play buried up to her waist and the rest of it up to her neck. What was the attraction of such a demanding part?
I'm delighted by Winnie, she's very intriguing for lots of reasons. She has very nice, very Irish aspects, such as her desire to be high-minded, whereas in his growing degradation her husband Willie seems to have given up, so she seems to be living with a brute beast. I'm also moved that Beckett chose to put a woman in this situation. Disappointment and hope are things that flash much more across a woman's face than a man's. I was walking down the street the other day and I thought, every woman looks like Winnie – in the way they button up their coats hopefully, wear high heels to give themselves height hopefully, yet at the same time have a little look of disappointment in their faces.

How are you and your director Deborah Warner approaching her in rehearsal?
I made a mound, with a table and sandbags, and got into it. I did a play recently when I was in bed all day and it really demoralised me. So every hour I get out and play badminton. That's what's kept my spirits up. I have a text with the words only. Deborah has the stage directions. She interrupts me with the directions, so I hear rather than read them, which is much better. She has a music stand, so she's almost conducting me.
How does she best help you as a director?
She hears what I hear: musically we're very similar. She knows when things run out of energy, she's terribly good on rhythm. She's also very accurate; she doesn't give me a single note that's irrelevant. She picks me up on my faults, she hears the bum notes in my delivery. She's very assured and that gives me confidence.
Do you find it necessary to delve into the meaning of every sentence?
You delve when you have a problem. When you yield to the text, it stops having many mysteries. Beckett has imagined something quite simple. He's emptied Winnie's and Willie's brains of all the things that fill our lives, and left the fact that she doesn't want to speak only to herself. She needs to be witnessed, and love and witness are very connected.
What about the language itself?
I'm very delighted by it. Winnie speaks a very public language, even though the thoughts are fragmentary. It's not mumbling, it's very particular. If the phrases become too realistic, they become boring. People think that by making Beckett ordinary you find the key. But you don't, because it's *extra*ordinary. Whereas Shakespeare explains to you the picture he paints, Beckett paints a picture in your mind without explaining it. As soon as you've got a picture he cuts it; he won't let you linger in some sentimental memory.
Does being Irish make any difference to your playing of the part?
I do hear a lot of these phrases as quotes from Oliver St John Gogarty or Yeats that English people wouldn't necessarily get. But I've got to be careful that I'm not seduced by the tone being Irish, just because it sounds right.

Happy Days opened in the Lyttelton in January 2007.

Political, personal and magical

Tom Cairns and his actors share their thoughts about Brian Friel's *Aristocrats*

Tom Cairns / Director

It's a roller-coaster ride of a play and a great subject that it sits inside: in this case the relatively small Roman Catholic aristocracy, rather than the normal Anglo-Irish Protestant ascendancy. Friel is talking about the human condition, how people interact, how families are with each other, and sometimes the dysfunctional nature of their relationships.

There's a very Chekhovian side to the play, where you have a lot of thoughts and feelings that are unspoken. We spent the first week of rehearsal talking a great deal about the relationships. There was so much to discuss about this family, so much history and so much damage that had been done to all the children in one way or another. So we needed to thrash out what kind of responsibility each character wanted to take for their own condition. But because the writing is very strong and focused, it didn't take long to come to a consensus on such matters.

It's very much an ensemble piece: you often have seven or eight people on stage, with only maybe two of them speaking at one time. So a lot of ensemble directing has to go on; you have to make sure that everyone is alive when they're not speaking. That needs very careful handling.

Peter McDonald / Eamon

What is great about Brian Friel's plays is that you can approach them from almost any level, whether it's the political, personal or magical, or even musical, because he has an amazing ability to make a play almost sound like music. Some characters recur in his work, but in very subtle ways. My character Eamon is the classic Frielian outsider. He's an extremely intelligent man, who's aware of the political and historical ramifications of his class, but at the same time he understands their humanity in the sunset of their era.

When you do a big ensemble piece like this, you have to keep your eye on everyone else's story. That's very good for an actor, because often you can get too wrapped up in your own character's story. This piece demands that you throw yourself into the milieu, which means the themes of the play start to resonate earlier in rehearsal than they would normally do.

Dervla Kirwan / Alice

The play shows how a tyrannical father can cause so much destruction, how these people use fantasy to protect themselves, and to protect what is clearly falling around their ears. Alice is an alcoholic: her anxiety, her insecurity, her low self-esteem are laid out at various points. But for an actress to gather all that up and yet not labour it is quite a challenge. To do drunk acting is very difficult – I've seen some very bad examples. I think the trick is to underplay it, but I also have to embrace the size of the Lyttelton.

With this kind of ensemble piece you have to be especially in tune with the other actors. But there's something comforting about having a lot of other people on stage with you. It's complicated for the director, but Tom has never made it feel that way; he's pointed us very delicately in the direction he wants us to go.

Andrew Scott / Casimir

The play has some of the exquisite agony of Chekhov. It's about how we tell lies to each other and to ourselves in order to survive. I think we all do that to a certain extent, but in the play it's quite extreme. Yet there's a huge amount of love within it. And because the characters are so strong and alive, it's also very funny, though not in an obvious way.

I saw the play at the Gate in Dublin when I was about ten, and the character I remember most is Casimir. The most appealing thing about him is his vulnerability, and the fact that he's incapable of disguising it when something punctures his life. That's why his family love him. He's also somebody who is very much himself. We keep finding out new things about him, discovering what he says simply to please other people and what is actually true.

Gina McKee / Judith

Like all brilliant playwrights, Brian Friel lets the details of his characters' histories and their unspoken complexities leak and spill out in a way that draws you right in. To have the chance to explore their histories and pick up the clues he has given us in *Aristocrats* is a real pleasure. It helps greatly that as director Tom approaches the play in a very informal way, effortlessly making people feel they can contribute. It's a skill we don't credit as much as we should.

In the case of my character Judith, the power of duty within her is very evident in the play, but I think she may actually be using it to mask other elements in her life, which she should really be questioning. The glimpses you get of those elements are rare, but they are very poignant when you find them.

Aristocrats opened in the Lyttelton in July 2005.

A lovable but complicated man

Martha Clarke is directing Christopher Hampton's play about Lewis Carroll and Alice Liddell

'There will be people who come expecting a Tenniel kind of atmosphere – but they're not going to get it,' Martha Clarke says emphatically, relaxing at the end of the first week's rehearsals of *Alice's Adventures Under Ground*. What, then, can audiences at the National expect from her direction of the play (the title is the original one for *Alice In Wonderland*), on which this American choreographer and director has collaborated with playwright Christopher Hampton? 'It won't be like *The Wind in the Willows*, with tails and whiskers and all that,' she explains. 'It'll be more of a keyhole view of Victorian life. I'm trying to get a balance between humour, menace and despair.'

Although the play centres on Lewis Carroll's famous Alice stories, it's essentially about the real-life relationship between the Oxford mathematics don Charles Dodgson (Carroll's real name) and the young Alice Liddell. It looks at the darker, repressed side of a man who never made any adult emotional attachments, who was obsessed with photographing young girls, and whose psychological make-up has been the subject of intense debate over the years. 'He was a lovable but complicated man,' Clarke suggests, a view she's arrived at after having read several biographies of Dodgson from different periods. 'Those pictures have a great melancholy. I think he was in love with Alice, whatever that means. She was his muse, the source of his creativity.'

Choreography apart, although she's directed many operas and multimedia shows around the world, this is the first time she's directed a straight text. 'I've got such good actors, each day is a revelation,' she confesses. 'I'm frightened to be enjoying it so much.' The project came about almost by accident. She had asked Hampton if he would adapt a short novel for her music-theatre company. He read it and declined, but asked if she had anything else up her sleeve. 'I said, "Yes, Alice" – though I didn't really.' The project was born. (Was it a coincidence that Hampton's eldest daughter is also called Alice?) The early work was done in the National's Studio. Initially she, Hampton and the actors simply played around with Carroll's famous stories. It was only when Dodgson himself came into the frame that the play began to take shape.

The delicate subject matter has prompted the National not to recommend the play for children under twelve. Yet the young girl playing Alice, Sasha Hanau, is only nine, and has been working on and off on the part for two years. How has she coped with the adult discussions in rehearsals? 'On the one hand she's uncannily sophisticated and gets everything,' Clarke explains. 'She's like Alice herself, the voice of reason. But she also has a kind of protection around her – and what she doesn't get doesn't matter.' In directing the play she's convinced there's no need to make concessions to a teenage audience. 'At that age young people are often far more hip than grown-ups or critics,' she says. 'There's no need to pander to them.'

Alice's Adventures Under Ground opened in the Cottesloe in November 1994.

A young man's play

Simon Russell Beale returns to Stoppard's
Rosencrantz and Guildenstern Are Dead

Simon Russell Beale is no stranger to the play that shot Tom Stoppard to fame. The role of Guildenstern, which he is playing in the National's new production, is one he tackled at school in Bristol at the age of sixteen. 'It was an unusual choice for a school play and I loved it,' he says. 'I'd done almost entirely Shakespeare and a bit of Sheridan, so it was a great release to do such a different kind of drama. I remember especially the sheer thrill of the question-and-answer game the two of them play: it was just like the feeling of skateboarding.'

He was attracted to the idea of revisiting the part because of the technical challenges of the play, but also because over the last three years he's tended to play very dark parts, notably Richard III, Konstantin in *The Seagull* and Edward II with the Royal Shakespeare Company, and Mosca in *Volpone* at the National. 'I've got used to being unlikeable,' he says. So what, as a grown-up professional, does he bring to the role now? 'I think it needs a certain elan, an effervescence, and I rather pride myself on my speed of thought. It's not a particularly physical role, but it's the nearest to me of any of the parts I've played recently.'

He believes *Rosencrantz and Guildenstern Are Dead* – Stoppard's first stage play, written in 1966 – is very much a young man's piece, full of a young man's conceits. 'But the trick is that it's also very sad, because you get to like Rosencrantz and Guildenstern, and it's about the distress that they go through and the idea of life just disappearing, of death being nothing.'

Rosencrantz and Guildenstern Are Dead opened in the Lyttelton in December 1995.

Familiar territory

Stella Gonet is playing an idealistic schoolteacher in David Hare's *Skylight*

While David Hare's play was widely acclaimed by the critics when it was first performed at the National two years ago, there was less unanimity about the motives and character of Kyra, the idealistic schoolteacher working with children in the East End of London.

Some admired her passionately held convictions and saw her motives for working with those at the 'bottom of the pile' as generally pure. Others saw her as a woman driven by guilt, or by a need for self-sacrifice: one labelled her 'a priggish and smug self-appointed angel of mercy'. Stella Gonet is playing Kyra (with Bill Nighy as Tom) in the National's current touring production, again directed by Richard Eyre. Talking just before rehearsals begin, she emphasises the positive elements of the character, while admitting that her perspective might change once she begins to explore the play in more detail.

'I have a great admiration for Kyra, she's doing something that is very noble, and that's what I want to push to the front,' she says. 'But two days in the rehearsal room and all that might go straight out the window.' The territory that Kyra works in is not unfamiliar to her. Her mother is a teacher and her sister runs a charity for children in the East End, for which she herself has occasionally worked. 'I know a bit about what goes on there,' she says. This family link to education and children may explain why she doesn't feel the need to do any research into teachers' lives or their working conditions. 'The danger in doing that is that you would then feel you were representing a particular group of people and that you might let them down,' she says.

Stella Gonet is familiar with David Hare's work, having played the main female role in the National's first production of *Racing Demon* in 1990. She believes he's one of the few male writers who can provide good challenging roles for women. 'I love him for writing these parts, I think he has an incredible understanding of women and admires them a lot,' she says. 'In his plays he often gives them his most heartfelt speeches – as he does with Kyra, when she attacks those who criticise teachers' motives and judgement from the safety of offices of Parliament, but never lift a finger themselves.'

She sees *Skylight* as a beautiful chamber piece. 'I haven't read anything so good for a long time, and Kyra is a role that any actress would leap at. But the writing is very delicate, it's like Chekhov; so you have to be careful to keep the balance right between the characters. It's a big challenge, it demands real grown-up acting.' She clearly identifies strongly with Kyra's character. 'I like to think that, like her, I have a lot of hope and faith in the future, and a lot of energy and spirit. I do often seem to play women who have a message to put over, or who have a strong vocational urge.'

Skylight toured during spring and early summer 1997.

A universal struggle

Jochum Ten Haaf on playing the young Van Gogh in *Vincent in Brixton*

It seemed like a dream come true when I got the part of Van Gogh in Nicholas Wright's play. I had just graduated and I was thinking about my future life, how maybe in twenty years' time I would act abroad, maybe even in the West End. And now that the play has transferred from the National Theatre, it's happened already.

What I found so fascinating with the script was that it told of a nineteen-year-old boy's struggle to find his way. And that's so universal, that's something everybody goes through. Vincent is interchangeable with any boy of that age, with his hormones working, and falling in love. I thought this was a better approach to his character than thinking, 'What will people expect when they see Van Gogh?' Normally, when you think of him you get a romantic image, you see sunflowers and sunsets and fields. But that's not very interesting, because that's what we already know, whereas the play is about an obscure period of his life. He's an art dealer, he's posh and well-off, he says: 'I don't have any talent.' All that is so nice to play with.

Richard Eyre gets the best out of actors and that's a great gift in a director. He gives you confidence, he's very calm, he creates the perfect atmosphere to work in. He's not pushy or aggressive or impatient, and he trusts you to try things out. The first thing he said to me was, 'You're always commenting on the character, instead of just being Vincent and doing what he does. Let the audience decide what to make of it – is it funny, is it stupid, is it laughable?' That was very valuable to me. What I found difficult was not to try to be liked. I think in the end you feel sympathy for Vincent, but he's not a sympathetic character like Sam Plowman – he's the one the audience can relate to, because he's so likeable; Vincent is rude, he doesn't have any social skills. But as an actor you want the audience to root for your character, so I want to be charming. Richard has to restrain me.

Claire Higgins is amazing to play opposite. She makes other people's performances better, instead of just concentrating on her own. So when I'm doing a scene with her I'm at my most relaxed, because it's almost as if I don't have to do anything; I just listen and that's nearly enough. She's such a big presence and yet she doesn't dominate, she shares the stage with you and that's really good.

Vincent in Brixton opened in the Cottesloe in May 2002.

Beyond the rich bitch

Harriet Walter on playing the hostess from hell in
Moira Buffini's *Dinner*

She has tackled several meaty roles in her time: Lady Macbeth,
the Duchess of Malfi, Hedda Gabler, to name but three of the
toughest. So it's a surprise to hear from Harriet Walter that she
thinks Paige in Moira Buffini's savage new play *Dinner* is one
of the hardest she's played so far.

'Like Hedda and Lady Macbeth, she has an inner secret, a
reason for the poison inside, which is never explained to the
audience,' she says, as we talk during rehearsals. 'Without
giving the plot away, Paige will be understood only at the end
of the evening. The challenge is to keep the audience interested
enough to work her out retrospectively.' Intelligent, cynical
and savagely witty, Paige is the hostess from hell, bent on
giving the ultimate dinner party. But Harriet Walter is keen to
get beyond the rich bitch she might seem at first reading. 'You
have to find a character's humanity if you're going to live with
her for weeks,' she says. 'With Paige it's all there, the text gives
you many mystifying moments to play with.'

She conducted a similar investigation when she played Lady
Macbeth for the Royal Shakespeare Company in 1999, an
experience she recorded recently in a short but insightful book.
But she's keen to stress that for her Paige is not simply a
variation on her 'classical sisters' in Ibsen and Shakespeare. 'I
suppose there's a pond down there that breeds something in a
similar area, but I hate feeling I'm going into old territory.
Also, people say characters like Lady Macbeth and Hedda
Gabler are cold and calculating, whereas I think I have a gene
missing about coldness – I just don't have it. And Paige is not
at all like me, so I'm looking to other role models, to a mixture
of people I know.'

A versatile and subtle actress who has succeeded in a wide
range of parts new and old, she confesses to being a very
'driven' person. In her book on *Macbeth* she writes: 'There is a
fury inside me somewhere; there is a hunger, and maybe even

the capacity to kill.' Perhaps it's this mixture of qualities that compels her to throw herself wholeheartedly into rehearsals, as she clearly has done with *Dinner*. 'I know it's only a social satire, but you still have to go in deep,' she says. 'There's a lot of talk about death, a lot of rather cynical, hate-filled stuff, so you can get quite depressed. Not in a Stanislavsky way: but just as if you think long enough about a delicious meal you start to salivate, so if you think long enough about death and hate, you start to crumble. But if you're a serious actor you do have to confront life and death issues. You also have to think, "This could be me." That's the little slogan I put before every part I play.'

The director of *Dinner* is Fiona Buffini, the writer's sister. 'She and Moira seem to see eye to eye and understand each other's mind,' she observes. 'They have an enormous respect for each other.' She very much approves of Fiona's directorial style. 'She keeps up a good jokey atmosphere and lets us share problems, but she knows when to plough on. It's a good combination.'

She's fascinated to observe how women directors have changed. 'In the 1970s there were only a few and they were rather embattled. You were supposed to be loyal to them because they were women, trying to break the mould of male authority. That could result in emotional blackmail, whereas the men would use threats. The new generation like Fiona are much more confident and at ease with their authority. They take the play by the horns, and that's really stimulating.'

Dinner opened in the temporary Loft Theatre in November 2002.

Rigour with freedom

Peter Gill discusses *Scenes from the Big Picture* and his way of working with actors

Some directors know before they start rehearsals how they want to shape a play. Others trust that working with actors will unlock its secrets. Peter Gill, once an actor himself, belongs to the latter school. 'I'm not a conceptual director, I can never make up my mind beforehand what a play is about,' he says. 'Only as I work on it do things emerge.'

He's just started rehearsing *Scenes from the Big Picture*, Owen McCafferty's powerful new play, which weaves together transforming moments in the lives of twenty characters during one summer's day in Belfast. So what has he pulled out of the work so far? 'I'm finding that it's a play dominated by marriage and other male–female relationships: the old couple, the young girl trying to find the right boy, and all gradations in between. The other strong element is people's powerlessness. It's quite a celebratory play, but also quite a sad one.'

Like Owen McCafferty's earlier work such as *Closing Time*, his new play doesn't focus on the troubled politics of Northern Ireland, though they are implicitly there in the background. This appeals to Gill. 'It challenges the audience to watch a piece about Belfast that doesn't reduce people's lives to an item on *Newsnight*,' he says. Another attraction is the language. McCafferty uses several dialect and slang words, but also writes 'in the accent', producing rich, earthy dialogue that roots the characters in their daily lives. 'At first you think it's a documentary, to which you bring various prejudices – because of the characters' class, because of the setting,' Gill suggests. 'In fact, it's very patterned writing, and language ideas keep recurring.'

Peter Gill's mother's family were Irish, and his productions include *Juno and the Paycock* for the National and *Uncle Vanya* adapted by Frank McGuinness for Field Day, as well as a filmed version of Joyce's short story *Grace*, and *Fugitive*, a television play about a Catholic priest. Yet he claims not to be especially drawn to Irish work (his own background is Welsh working-class). What he clearly is drawn to are plays in dialect, most famously the three D. H. Lawrence plays he directed at the Royal Court in the 1960s. 'I've even done one set in Northamptonshire,' he says. With McCafferty's play he's not gone for an all-Irish company. Although most of the actors are Irish born or bred, Scotland, Wales and Lancashire are also represented. 'I've always gone for the actor, not the accent,' he observes. With the young actors playing the four teenage roles – two each from Dublin and Belfast – he's brought in an Irish voice teacher. 'They have this quick, demotic speech, so she's been helping them not to be over-speedy.'

Given the play's forty scenes, he first asked the actors to read them in an arbitrary order, making a collage of stories, before reading them in the right sequence. 'I work more closely with the actors than some directors do,' he says. 'It's a question of knowing the difference between one actor and another, and knowing when to let the slack out. So I use a mixture of quite close work springing from the needs of the text, and something more intuitive based on people's perceptions of each other. Two methods running in parallel, one rather rigorous and one much freer.'

Despite being a writer himself – his play *The York Realist* attracted rave reviews last year – he prefers when directing to have the writer come in at the start of rehearsals, but not much thereafter. 'I believe the actors should be free to ask questions that would seem irrelevant to the writer,' he argues. 'Sometimes the play has to be talked about impertinently, without anyone having to censor themselves.' He's also opposed to the idea of altering a text in rehearsal, which he believes can simply add the director's flaws to the writer's. 'There's a cult of plays being there to be rewritten,' he says. 'But then they become scripts, not plays.'

Scenes from the Big Picture opened in the Cottesloe in April 2003.

One of the peacock people

Robert Lindsay is enjoying playing a corrupt politician in Nick Dear's *Power*

Power is a beautifully written play, I think it's up there with the great works like Peter Shaffer's *Amadeus*. Although the notices have been excellent, if there has been a criticism it is that it doesn't have enough modern resonances. I think there are some, but it's not a modern political thriller, it's an historical story. Nick Dear has researched it wonderfully well, so that every historical detail is authentic.

The part of Nicholas Fouquet, superintendent of finance to Louis XIV, I found irresistible: I had no hesitation in accepting it as soon as I read the script. I certainly saw a few modern parallels to him, such as Peter Mandelson and Jeffrey Archer, peacock people who overfamiliarise themselves with those in power, then go too far. I don't think we'll ever unravel the machinations of politicians, they're so complex and corrupt.

Fouquet himself is dreadfully corrupt, but he was a man who genuinely loved the society he was in, and he didn't actually mean any harm. He did charge a bit too much interest on his loans, but he was incredibly generous, he lived for beauty and pleasure, and he was an important patron of writers, including Molière. His downfall came because of his jealousy of Louis.

He's also, I think, a more interesting character because of his insecurity – he's actually a depressive. I suppose a lot of my roles are a mixture of razor-sharp comedy and vulnerability. I wanted to find something different in Fouquet, something much sourer, but both Nick Dear and our director Lindsay Posner, and also my own instincts, pushed me towards his vulnerability, which is clearly there in the text.

I love playing in period costume. Although *Power* is set in France, it's the time of the Restoration and Charles II in England. Restoration comedy has been my love and passion ever since I was at RADA. We also did a production of *The Rivals* there, under the guidance of some wonderful teachers, who taught me a tremendous amount.

I think the traverse shape we use in the Cottesloe is the perfect shape for a chamber work like *Power*, where most of the scenes are two-handers. It certainly suits me down to the ground; it allows you to parade up and down. It also means that being near, the audience captures every nuance, every mood change. I don't think I could have coped with Fouquet in the Olivier, or even in the Lyttelton's proscenium arch.

Power opened in the Cottesloe in July 2003.

Long night's journey

David Tennant on the demands of playing in *The Pillowman*

I thought Martin McDonagh's earlier plays were brilliantly funny and dazzlingly skilful. But none of them hit me the way *The Pillowman* did. I thought it was the best new play I'd come across in years. It didn't shock me, but I was aware it was pushing the envelope, that it was presenting uncommon theatrical fare and that it would shock some people.

Playing Katurian is exciting, but also tough. Firstly, being on stage all the time requires great concentration. Secondly, although it's not an especially physically demanding part, it's hard work because the journey you go on is so grim. But the thing about such good writing is that you can just surrender yourself to it. At the start of the play I try not to think about what's coming, about the vast distance I've got to travel. It's easy to do that with *The Pillowman*, because the scenes are so playable.

It's exciting to be in a new play that is this good, where you're telling the story for the first time. But with such a mentally gruelling part, I find the repertory system at the National a real joy. Doing eight shows a week can quickly squeeze the life out of you, but because here you have a few days' break, you come back each time feeling fresh. Of course that keeps it scary further into the run, but although that can be exhausting, it's good for the work.

It helps that John Crowley is such a good director. In rehearsals he's very calm and relaxed, he makes you feel that he's the captain of the ship, but that you have the freedom to discover things for yourself. You feel you can try anything, but that you can trust him absolutely to give you the right guidance. That's the kind of rehearsal process that gets the best out of actors.

Martin McDonagh was in rehearsals and he was a very good resource. There were things that he had an opinion on, things that he wanted to be sure we were getting right. Sometimes it can be stifling to have the writer there, but it was good to feel he was behind every word, that we had his stamp of approval. There are questions about how certain things happened before the play begins, which the audience don't need to understand, but which the actors do. That was something Martin was happy for us to discover for ourselves. But there's a lot of second guessing as to what may or may not be true, where he would intervene if he felt we were making the wrong assumptions.

I'm lucky to be in such a Rolls-Royce company. Working with someone like Jim Broadbent is a delight, but it's very hard not to laugh. At one point he tells the story of a Chinese boy, which I never managed to get through until the dress rehearsal without laughing. Even now I have to dig weals in my hand with my fingernails to stop myself cracking up. He's just so funny, even when he's being serious, and it's very difficult not to be affected by that.

The Pillowman opened in the Cottesloe in November 2003.

Avoiding impersonation

How did Nicholas Farrell and Alex Jennings prepare for playing Tony Blair and George W. Bush in David Hare's *Stuff Happens*?

Having to play a real character on stage is always a challenge for an actor. It's tricky enough when they're famous but dead. When they're such recognisable living and breathing figures as Tony Blair or George W. Bush, it's something else again.

So how do you best prepare for such a part? How far do you go down the road of impersonation? Given that audiences will

uch a technically complex show, with large pieces of
y flying in and out or rising up and down, he says the cast
had to keep their wits about them. 'Everyone has
ed the set now, but it's amazing what actors are
ed to do. The technicians have seen it all before, but
you're pushed out on a ledge with a twenty-foot drop
ked to stand still, you can't help feeling frightened at

ving recently become a father, he's fascinated to see how
en are responding to *His Dark Materials*. 'It's amazing,
days when we play both parts, that after five and a half
you find six-year-old kids still glued to what's happening
ge. That's a fantastic first taste of theatre and they'll go
or the rest of their lives. It's great that the National is
them such a wonderful experience.'

ark Materials opened in the Olivier in December 2003.

itical and playful

ickson is directing *The Hothouse*, the
ing-link play' in the Pinter canon

lay in 1954 Harold Pinter turned up at the Maudsley in
on. The hospital wanted volunteers to act as guinea pigs
experiment. The pay was ten shillings. Pinter needed
oney. Without explanation, they put him in a room with
odes. Suddenly he heard a terrible noise through the
ones. After a few seconds it was switched off. It left him
bling all over. It was an experience he would never
.

erwards, when he asked the staff what it was all about,
said they were testing levels of reaction. 'That mystified
he recalled. 'Who exactly were they going to give this kind
ck treatment to? Anyway, *The Hothouse* was kicked off by
experience. I was well aware of being used for an
iment, and feeling quite powerless.'

be familiar with the witty attacks on such figures by Rory
Bremner or John Culshaw of *Dead Ringers*, how do you avoid
satirising them? These were the questions facing Nicholas
Farrell and Alex Jennings as they talked during rehearsals for
Stuff Happens, David Hare's revealing new play about the
political manoeuvrings in the lead-up to the invasion of Iraq.

Farrell admits that he hesitated when first offered the Blair
role. 'I'm not a mimic in any conventionally accepted sense
and I don't look at all like him,' he says. 'The only living person
I've played before is Alan Bennett in *The Lady in the Van*, and
he's got such a unique voice, that was rather different.' He cites
Michael Sheen's portrayal of Blair in the TV drama *The Deal*
as a good example of an actor avoiding caricature.

Although he acknowledges the problem of the TV satirists,
whose work he's been looking at, he points out that their sole
intention is to make you laugh at Blair. 'The idea in the play is
to give a strong flavour of his character, but not to mimic him.
If you do that, people stop listening to the play and start
thinking about how you've used a gesture or managed some
piece of phrasing. And that's counter-productive: you've got a
wonderful history play here, and every word of it is worth
listening to.'

One of the pleasures of the part is that it gives him an
opportunity to confound people's expectations. 'You might be
expecting wide eyes, a big smile and boyish enthusiasm, but
that's only a tiny part of Blair. We only see him in interviews,
or making speeches at press conferences, at party conferences,
or in the House of Commons. But in the play, as in his private
life, he gets angry, frustrated and upset. So we get a side of him
we don't normally see.'

In tackling the part of George W. Bush, Alex Jennings also
aims to reach beyond popular conceptions, in this instance that
of an unintelligent, linguistically challenged president. 'One
attraction of the role is that he doesn't say much, and you have
to decide whether there's something going on behind the face,
or nothing. I think there *is* something and that David's portrait
of him makes sense; he's grown into his role. He's not a fool,
he wouldn't have got that far if he were.'

In his research he's avoided the satirists, but watched again Bush's speeches and press conferences. 'Without impersonating him, you've got to suggest something. In rehearsal I'm making a stab at getting his Texan accent right and looking at the way he moves physically. I can't yet do the walk and the talk at the same time: you think you've got it in the morning, but by the end of the day it's disintegrated.'

As when he played the title role in David Edgar's *Albert Speer*, he's found that he understands Bush much better after reading about his life; his faith, his drinking, the effect on him of the death of his sister. 'You may not approve of these characters or their beliefs, but it's interesting to see how the pieces of the jigsaw fit together to make them who they are. As an actor I have to empathise with some part of Bush.'

At the start of rehearsals director Nicholas Hytner asked the actors to observe one house rule: leave your politics outside the rehearsal room. Farrell apparently hasn't found this a problem. 'The fact that I disagree with Tony Blair on some issues is just not a factor,' he says. Intriguingly, Jennings seems less certain: 'It's not easy to put your politics aside and I don't think we do, really.'

Stuff Happens opened in the Olivier in September 2004.

Archetypal man

David Harewood is enjoying his commanding role in Philip Pullman's *His Dark Materials*

He is a powerful presence on stage and that's the way he likes it. 'There's so much cerebral acting around, whenever I get a chance I try to put as much physicality into a part as possible,' David Harewood says. 'I like to give people their money's worth. I want them to sit up and take notice.'

They did so when he played Othello at the National seven years ago. And he's certainly grabbing the attention in the current revival of *His Dark Materials*, where he's taken on the

part of Lord Asriel, played last year by Tim[...] stamped it with his own vigorous, swashbuc[...] Asriel is a fantastically engaging character a[...] matic,' he says, as we talk between shows. 'F[...] man – uncaring and insensitive, but also a[...] He's got laser-beam concentration and gr[...] him as embodying the true spirit of the Engli[...] valour and strength.'

From the beginning he knew that he wan[...] a different take from that of his predecesso[...] production it was all woolly jumpers and [...] wanted to move away from that, make him [...] sexy – hence the leather trousers. I also wa[...] more physical, which meant I sometimes [...] fighting with three or four people at the sam[...] read Philip Pullman's trilogy of novels befor[...] offered him the part of Asriel, and was bov[...] did so. 'I was amazed that such a fantastic[...] out of his head.' He also found the books u[...] for finding out more about the characters w[...] driven stage version, have inevitably to be [...] strokes.

He admits to being affected in a differe[...] about the struggles Philip Pullman had in [...] was inspiring to read about the difficul[...] background, about not knowing his fathe[...] into storytelling almost by accident, then [...] education. It was an inspiration to me [...] difficult backgrounds can rise to the top lik[...]

Much of the rehearsal time for the re[...] *Materials* was inevitably spent on the more [...] – especially those featuring bears and witch[...] the daemons right. This left less time t[...] straightforward 'acting' scenes, a situatic[...] admits left him feeling anxious. 'It was a b[...] was amazing how quickly it came togethe[...] Nick helped us to paint our characters and [...] the scenes were about.'

Like *The Birthday Party* and *The Dumb Waiter*, the play concerns the oppression of the individual by malignant forces, in this case the staff of a so-called 'rest home', where the inmates are known by numbers rather than names, and the staff themselves dehumanised under the malign leadership of the unpredictable Roote. Its history is interesting. Pinter initially saw it as a radio play and, uncharacteristically, produced a synopsis for the BBC in 1958. But after *The Birthday Party* received a famously critical drubbing, he put it aside 'for further deliberation'. In 1979 he re-read it, decided it was worth staging and directed the first production himself the following year at the Hampstead Theatre.

The National's new production is by Ian Rickson, until recently artistic director at the Royal Court. Last year he directed Pinter there in Beckett's *Krapp's Last Tape*, where they evidently established a good working relationship. 'I found him very supple and responsive as an actor,' he says, as we talk between auditions for the National production. 'He was very open to any processes I used. It was such a pleasure.' He believes it's a good moment for a revival of what he calls Pinter's 'missing-link play', one that is relatively unknown in the Pinter canon. 'It's clairvoyant, anticipating the later plays in dealing with totalitarianism, with the individual being crushed by the powers-that-be. But it also has the early work's imaginative playfulness.'

Ironically, this very political play was written at a time when Pinter was perceived as essentially non-political. Yet despite the terrifying material it contains and its Kafkaesque nightmarish quality, it has all the ingredients of a black farce. With his own brand of surreal humour Pinter exposes the ever-shifting aims and desires of his characters, often using the kind of cross-talk repartee that belonged to the music-hall tradition. ('How do you know what mothers look like?' – 'I had one myself.')

Rickson is in no doubt about the play's relevance nearly fifty years after Pinter first conceived it. 'It has a very contemporary feel,' he says. 'It's looking at a world that is excessively hierarchical, fearful, masculine, at an institution that destroys not only the people housed there, but also those that run it. It doesn't take much of an imaginative leap to think of correspondences today.'

He underlines the challenge that actors face in working on a Pinter play. 'They require real intensity and bravery. Underneath the surface they need a density of feeling and the articulation of high stakes, while on the surface they have to cover it, control it with rigour and discipline. It requires total immersion in the hatred, fear, panic and longing, yet the ability to play his musical cadences and focused language with absolute clarity. And that's demanding.' He believes some of the characters in *The Hothouse* have qualities to be found in their creator, who himself played Roote in a revival at Chichester in 1995, which then went into the West End. 'There's the anarchic Lush, who won't be bound by any rules, and the young pup Lamb, who's full of open and individualistic urges. These seem to me to be versions of Harold.'

Pinter himself has taken an active part in auditions, and plans to be present at rehearsals. 'To have him involved like this is lovely, and very helpful,' Rickson says. 'In a way it's like being back at the Royal Court, with the writer absolutely part of the whole process.'

The Hothouse opened in the Lyttelton in July 2007.